More Praise for
ZEN BRIDGE

"Grace and Peter Schireson have offered a treasure to the world in the form of an introduction to their teacher, the renowned Rinzai Zen master Keido Fukushima Roshi. Each spare talk in his simple, lucid English is like a shaving planed from a block of flawless cedar—aromatic, deeply grained, and luminous. I leave it feeling as if I've spent a great night with a new friend and a great Zen teacher."
—HOSHO PETER COYOTE, Zen priest and author of *Sleeping Where I Fall*

"Keido Fukushima is one of the signal Rinzai masters of our times. Within this wonderful anthology of his teachings, we can feel the twinkle in his eye and the constant pointing to the deep in a way rarely as inviting as we find here."
—JAMES ISHMAEL FORD, author of *If You're Lucky, Your Heart Will Break*

"In a manner that few books offer, this volume allows both the beginner and the advanced student to see into the realities of Zen practice."
—POLLY YOUNG-EISENDRATH, PHD, author of *The Present Heart*

"When the Heart Is Clear, the Hundred Tasks Go Well"

Calligraphy by Keido Fukushima

ZEN
BRIDGE

The Zen Teachings of
KEIDO
FUKUSHIMA
ROSHI

EDITED BY
Grace Schireson
& Peter Schireson

FOREWORD BY Barbara Ruch

Wisdom Publications
199 Elm Street
Somerville, MA 02144 USA
wisdompubs.org

Library of Congress Cataloging-in-Publication Data

Names: Fukushima, Keido, 1933– author. | Schireson, Grace Jill, editor. | Schireson,
    Peter, editor.
Title: Zen bridge: the Zen teaching of Keido Fukushima Roshi / edited by Grace
    Schireson & Peter Schireson.
Description: Somerville, MA: Wisdom Publications, 2017. | Includes index.
Identifiers: LCCN 2016031573| ISBN 9781614291978 (pbk.: alk. paper) | ISBN
    1614291977 (pbk.: alk. paper) | ISBN 9781614292142 (ebook) | ISBN 1614292140
    (ebook)
Subjects: LCSH: Zen Buddhism.
Classification: LCC BQ9266 .F839 2017 | DDC 294.3/420427—dc23
LC record available at https://lccn.loc.gov/2016031573

ISBN 978-1-61429-197-8   ebook ISBN 978-1-61429-214-2

21 20 19 18 17
5 4 3 2 1

Posture illustrations on pages 38–41 by Andrew Campbell.
Cover design by Barbara Haines. Interior design by Melissa Mykal Batalin. Set in
FF Scala 10.5/16.

Wisdom Publications' books are printed on acid-free paper and meet the guidelines
for permanence and durability of the Production Guidelines for Book Longevity of the
Council on Library Resources.

❦ This book was produced with environmental mindfulness.
For more information, please visit wisdompubs.org/wisdom-environment.

Printed in the United States of America.

MIX
Paper from
responsible sources
FSC® C005010

Please visit fscus.org.

Contents

II. MY ZEN TRAINING

III. ZEN MASTER JOSHU

IV. CLASSICAL TEACHING STORIES

Foreword

By Barbara Ruch

ZEN BRIDGE, edited by Grace and Peter Schireson, is a precious collection, in English translation, of teachings by the late Rinzai Zen master Keido Fukushima, chief abbot of Tofukuji monastery in Kyoto. The collection includes Abbot Fukushima's words on a wide range of themes—Zen mind, monastic life, the history of Buddhism, women in Zen, enlightenment, love, and many other topics—as shared with those who gathered to hear him both in his Kyoto monastery and in the U.S. It thereby fits succinctly into the long Chinese and Japanese historical tradition of the *goroku* genre, a record, by his disciples, of a master's spoken words.

The question of women in Zen Buddhism was the first link that bridged the work of an academic such as myself to the Zen master Keido Fukushima. During the 1980s, my research had been directed at exhuming the life of Mugai Nyodai (1226–1298), an extraordinary woman who became Japan's first female Zen master. I use the word *exhume* because she had been for all practical purposes buried by the subsequent maneuvering of male monks and the obliviousness of male historians. Evidence had emerged that early on she had sought to advance her Zen training at Tofukuji monastery, then newly founded by Abbot Enni Ben'en (1202–1280), who had just returned with cutting-edge Zen from his study in China. He was willing to take her on, but his male disciples caused a ruckus of opposition.

The denouement of Ben'en's dilemma remains unclear. Mugai Nyodai, however, undeterred, ultimately trained under the eminent Chinese Rinzai Zen monk Wu-hsüeh Tsü-yuan (J., Mugaku Sogen; 1226–1286) and was named by him as the official heir to his teaching. She became founding abbess of Keiaiji temple, designated later by shogunal decree to be the highest ranking temple of the female system of Five Mountain Convents in Kyoto. To Keido Fukushima, who was Ben'en's twentieth-century successor as head of Tofukuji, there was no dilemma; gender represented part of the history of Zen long overdue for rectification. Grace and Peter Schireson are living proof of the welcome he gave at Tofukuji to men and women alike in his *sesshin* and *koan* practices, and it was key to his belief in American Zen.

Though not a practitioner of Zen myself, I was blessed to know Keido Fukushima during his yearly visits to Columbia and later in Kyoto. At Tofukuji he played a vital role in both supporting our research efforts to ressurect the history of eminent nuns and in the founding of our Kyoto Center for the Study of Women, Buddhism, and Cultural History. He offered space and sustenance to our first team of scholars in our launch of research in the Imperial Buddhist Convents in Kyoto and Nara. He was my companion in revering Abbess Mugai Nyodai, and I know I have had my own life deeply influenced by his resonant Zen way of belief—empty of self, open, free, and generous, living joy, which is possible only when one is living in the present moment *now*. He himself simply *was*—no hashing over yesterday, no probing fears of tomorrow.

Whenever people who knew him well share memories, they usually end up mentioning that in his spare time on trips to new cities Abbot Fukushima always asked to travel over a local bridge he had not yet seen or crossed. What is it about bridges? Is it admiration for their architecture, their engineering? Is it the challenge to connect? Or is it simply some need to reach the other side? Perhaps it is awe at the full dimensions of what a bridge accomplishes? For Keido Fukushima one imagines all of the above, and more.

A bridge is one of the world's most powerful metaphors. Bridges are ubiquitous in virtually all cultures, fulfilling a very real and necessary function in everyday life. Americans are likely to envision the soaring steel of the Golden Gate, or the stalwart brick architecture of the Brooklyn Bridge. Our songs from childhood resonate with the names of bridges such as Avignon and London; history and legends hover ominously around bridges over the Rhine or the Kwai. In short, a bridge is more than its physical parts, and the who and the why of a Zen bridge has meaning for us all. The present book delivers the words of this major Japanese Zen master who was himself a kind of bridge; some background to his motivation and mission can help us understand the why.

To be human is to know joy and suffering. The latter is the heartfelt troublemaker, inherent in our species' angst and the source of our sense of vulnerability and longing for help. Notable "saviors" have appeared to us in the centuries who have shared their revelations or discoveries as to how to transcend the human condition of material, physical, and existential suffering. Siddhartha Gautama (the Buddha, or the Awakened One) in Nepal/ India around 560–480 B.C.E. was one; Jesus of Galilee (the Christ, or Son of God) another; and then Muhammad (God's Prophet) around 570–632 C.E. another, to name only three. Each taught a different way out of the pain of the human condition. Each was extraordinary and unique, yet very much a product of his age and the society into which he was born. Followers of Jesus and Muhammad formed their hegemonies in Mediterranean and European dominions. The insights to which Gautama had awakened spread East—Nepal, Tibet, Korea, China. In the context of Chinese civilization, Gautama's method of enlightenment and transcendence over suffering gained complex institutional manifestations, becoming highly scholarly and elite and also spreading popularly as a way to salvation from the pain of life. When the teachings crossed the narrow waters to the Japanese archipelago, a two-way tidal flow emerged with China as a mecca where Japanese scholar-monks could study evolving schools surrounding the Buddha's teachings, and Japan became rich soil where Chinese monks could plant the seeds of their teachings on Buddha's enlightenment.

At the extreme Eastern edge of the Asian continent, however, the Japanese islands, floating with the vast Pacific at their back, constituted a cul-de-sac. Interpretations of the Buddha whirlpooled there and flowered in uniquely Japanese ways, yet could go no farther, until science and technology made possible a neutralization of the barriers of space and time, and the Pacific could be bridged. Certainly the earliest serious figure to bridge the Pacific bearing Zen Buddhism across to America and beyond was D. T. Suzuki (1870–1966). A Japanese scholar of Buddhism, he was also a student of Western philosophy who had learned English as a youth from a Christian missionary, a competency later greatly enhanced by his Radcliffe-trained wife Beatrice Lane. His books in English on Zen, a discipline to which early on he was strongly attracted and which he practiced, became world-famous among philosophers and theologians. So famous that when late in life he lectured at Columbia University (1952–1957) he attracted avant-garde intellectuals, pioneer thinkers, and celebrities, among them psychoanalyst Erich Fromm and artists such as John Cage.

D. T. Suzuki was fully aware of the landmine problems inherent in explaining, on an intellectual level through essays and books, the essentially experiential nature of Rinzai Zen. And he was attempting to do so in English to boot. Trapped by the necessities of that language, with all its inclinations toward logic, rational categorization, and a fondness for dualisms, there can be no doubt that he strove hard to find in Rinzai Zen something in its processes on which the Western thinkers with whom he associated could chew. Abbot Fukushima, however, was no chewer. He was a biter. Take a bite. Taste the *now*. His playfully calligraphed message to Americans, "Watch, Touch, Bite," directed us to engage the present moment fully and freely. No slogging around in the past or mulling over the unknowable future. If he looked back, it was to admire his historic predecessors who had found enlightenment, such as the Chinese Zen monk Joshu who lived in the now with his freed-up mind.

Few knew that Keido Fukushima had spent his youthful monkhood as an intellectually curious student, who loved to read books and took more and more degrees in Buddhist history all the way through the doctorate. There could have been no greater shock to him, then, than to be told ultimately by his own Zen master that all of that was irrelevant to Zen enlightenment and was to be thrown away. A mind packed with all the various possible answers to dealing with the pain of life was itself simply a source of dilemma and vulnerability. The human mind and heart are beautiful things, most so when they cease baying at the moon, when emptied of clutter and open fully to the very time and place at hand: mindfulness, awareness, and oneness with the universe of this moment.

Keido Fukushima was fully aware of D. T. Suzuki's attempts to bridge, not just the Pacific, but the far wider psychological gulf in the Abrahamic West, where faith in an unseeable power in an unseeable world is considered the source of salvation from pain and is supported by texts under constant interpretation. Abbot Fukushima's own mentor, Zen Master Shibayama, was the one D. T. Suzuki recommended as his successor in bearing Zen Buddhism to the U.S. Then through that master to this disciple, the pressure of compassion was finally on for Fukushima himself to be that bridge in the 1980s.

America had by then morphed into a very different environment. People knew about Buddhism, or thought they did, but twentieth-century Buddhism there had become a strange conglomeration of mysticism and romantic attraction to the exotic East, reflective of the diverse lineages and practices and personalities of Buddhist teachers who came to America from around Asia. The menu of individual practices to choose from was extensive, and meditating, chanting, martial arts, and so on were taken to be what it was all about. Zen meditation morphed into a "meditation industry" of goods and services, equipment, and "mindfulness," sold like gym classes or one-minute mindfulness sessions online. For academics, of course, the enterprise was structured to seek and find answers in books. Even "correct" answers to koan were being published, to the astonishment of those who understood what the *process* of koan encounter was designed to achieve.

Two things about his motivations in crossing the Pacific were clear to those who knew Keido Fukushima. First, for him, Zen was not up for redesign, compromise, or sale. Zen was nothing unless it was true to its essential roots—clean and disciplined. A half-hearted little bit of this and that, and you ended up with a garden of weeds. His Rinzai Zen was joyful, compassionate, and uncompromisingly reflective of the processes he had been taught to undertake and live by—diligent training to encounter enlightenment directly. At the same time (and this may seem contradictory), not unlike D. T. Suzuki, he believed that Zen Buddhism can and must evolve and perfect itself each time it experiences the friction of contact with a new cultural environment, a new age. It had been so since India, and since China, and on into Japan. Pre-chewing was not necessary for it to be nourishing. Nor should it dilute in fusion, but, as in mankind's evolution itself, the grating challenges of the environment led to an evolution in the ability to survive and flourish. For the youth of America—whose problems clearly showed malaise, disenchantment with their lot, and few inner tools—he knew the power of Zen could be transformative.

One of the greatest hopes he held out for Zen in American society was that gender equality could move from the lip-service of historic Zen masters in Asia to a greater reality. He had seen how it had so far failed to do so in Japan. In America, however, men and women were already further along in the trek to an even playing field. Zen teaches that enlightenment vanquishes all dualities, especially that of male and female. He expressed a longstanding concern for the strangely silent side of the history of women in Japanese Zen, and the current absence even of Rinzai Zen training centers for women clerics, despite the pressing need. In his Dharma talks he rarely made a theme of gender, but it was part of the point of his mission in America. If asked: Would the presence of women in his training sessions at Tofukuji monastery disturb the concentration of his resident monks? "No," was always his direct reply. His reverence and mine for thirteenth-century Zen abbess Mugai Ngodai was the bridge that spanned the cultural and spiritual distance between this Western academic woman and this incomparable Zen abbot. Once kindled, a relationship emerged that lasted several decades until his death.

Now, five years after he left us, *Zen Bridge* brings Keido Fukushima back to us, talking to us. His words light up the path to that place in the Zen mind where for all of us, as he made clear, "Every day is a good day."

Barbara Ruch is Professor Emerita of Japanese Literature and Culture at Columbia University. She is the founder and current director of the Institute for Medieval Japanese Studies: Japanese Cultural Heritage Initiatives, and has received many prizes for her pioneering work in various disciplines.

Editors' Introduction

By Grace Schireson and Peter Schireson

UNDERSTANDING THE IMPACT of Fukushima Roshi's teaching requires just one word: powerful. His power as a Zen teacher can be explained, but also, like the Zen he taught, the importance and impact of his teaching went beyond words. His power had many dimensions: it was physically palpable, personally intimate, truly authoritative, engaging in English, and authentically Rinzai Zen. Each dimension was itself potent. But taken together the experience of working with him was breathtaking and loving at the same time. With him we felt both blown away and connected by deep affection.

We were blown away at our very first meeting with Fukushima Roshi, instigated by Grace's desire to practice with him. We shared the experience of having the wind knocked out of us, but neither of us could pinpoint exactly how or when it had happened during the brief and polite meeting. Fukushima Roshi's power came straight from his Zen experience and jolted our Zen sensibilities. Grace likened it to the power of meeting Suzuki Roshi thirty years previously. She proclaimed after that first meeting with Fukushima Roshi, in reference to the great ninth-century Zen master, "Joshu is alive and well in Kyoto; he speaks English, takes Western students, and I am coming back to practice with him." Whatever impact this first meeting had on us, facing Fukushima Roshi in koan *dokusan* was considerably more earth shattering and continued to reverberate in our lives.

Fukushima Roshi's personality was charming. He had a terrific wit, even in English, and was considered one of Kyoto's great Zen treasures. He was delightful in conversation and knew how to welcome and engage Americans:

"I think Godiva chocolates may be better than *satori*."

"Even Dirty Harry has buddha nature."

"I love Joan Baez because of the way she takes care of her audience."

"The most important contribution of American Zen is its equal number of women Zen masters."

"American Zen will become a mighty tree."

These are only a few examples of how Fukushima Roshi would include lively and humorous comments in conversation and discussion with Americans. While visiting the United States he would call Grace on her cell phone and would send faxes about his schedule from Japan. He was intent on being savvy, communicative, and engaged with his American students in ways that they could appreciate.

He was also personally attentive to our emotional needs. He reminded Grace to take care of Peter when she came to Tofukuji for a meeting that Peter couldn't attend due to a cold. He sent his personal regrets when Grace's mother died, preventing Grace from attending sesshin with him in Arkansas. He also once admonished Grace for attempting to make a formal bow when her foot was injured and wrapped in a bandage. Seeing Peter out walking in Kyoto, he pulled over in his chauffeured limousine en route to a speaking engagement, lowered the window, grinned, and said, "Don't forget dokusan tonight at eight o'clock!" He found ways to make sesshin accessible to us and other foreigners when there were physical obstacles or language barriers. He made a point of giving us beautiful and unique gifts: calligraphy, sculpture, and ceramics. He explained that the *dana paramita* (generosity) meant giving actual things, not just teachings. He also acknowledged that he had learned this from his own teacher, Shibayama Zenkei.

In addition to his disarming charm, Roshi had a formal side, rooted in his status as a disciple of Shibayama Roshi and as the *kancho*, or chief abbot, of Tofukuji monastery and the Tofukuji sect. Shibayama Roshi, Fukushima's second master, is often referred to as the greatest Zen master of the twentieth century. Shibayama Roshi oversaw Fukushima Roshi's training in koans, in relating to Americans, and in refinement through calligraphy and manner. We were immediately overwhelmed by Fukushima Roshi's personal Zen power, but we only learned of his high status in the world of Zen through books after we had already begun training with him.

THE HISTORY OF Fukushima Roshi's position as Tofukuji Kancho is significant. In Japan temples had historically been ranked by the Shogunate. While the original list of the *Gozan*, the Five Mountains of Kyoto, changed from time to time, Tofukuji monastery was always on it. Maybe this is why Fukushima Roshi came to host a visit from Prince Charles to the temple. Tofukuji is the head temple of twenty-three subtemples in Kyoto and oversees 370 Tofukuji sect temples throughout Japan. Fukushima Roshi became chief abbot of the Tofukuji sect in 1980. Beyond his formal status, Fukushima Roshi was also considered one of the finest calligraphers in Japan; it was not uncommon for him to have a backlog of three thousand requests for calligraphy.

By the late 1970s, Fukushima Roshi had been invited to be head priest of Tofukuji at least four times, via requests to his root teacher, Okada Roshi. But Okada Roshi had refused all four requests. In 1979 seven monks in purple robes came to Hofukuji temple in Okayama to make a final request to Okada Roshi that he allow his disciple, Fukushima Keido, to become the teacher of the Tofukuji training hall (*senmon sodo*). According to master-disciple custom, Fukushima Roshi sat quietly in the meeting room at Hofukuji while the request to Okada Roshi was presented yet again. At the beginning of the meeting, as per protocol, Okada Roshi invited the high-ranking Tofukuji priests to be seated. But the most senior priest in their delegation, who was then chief abbot of Tofukuji, replied that they would not be seated until Okada Roshi agreed to their request and allowed his disciple to leave Hofukuji for a position at Tofukuji. In the face of this bold behavior, Okada Roshi agreed to reconsider, at which point the Tofukuji delegation took their seats. The seriousness of their request was further underlined when the most senior Tofukuji abbot sat below Okada Roshi and continued to request that Fukushima be released. On the next day, Okada Roshi assented to the Tofukuji delegation's request. It was later reported that Okada Roshi said: "I feel like my treasure was stolen from me." And years later, looking back, Fukushima Roshi himself said of the situation, "I was very much touched by my master's deep love for me."[1]

Most of our time with Fukushima Roshi was spent in sesshin, koan dokusan at Tofukuji monastery, or over tea before or after visits to Kyoto. Fukushima Roshi was fierce and powerful in dokusan, and warm and engaging over tea. We also attended a number of his talks and calligraphy demonstrations in the U.S. In addition, Grace interviewed and recorded Fukushima Roshi in Japan and in the U.S., and brought groups of her Zen students to visit Tofukuji, during which Fukushima Roshi lectured on Zen and answered their many questions with the help of Grace's translation. These talks were recorded as well.

Fukushima Roshi's U.S. visits continued the legacy of D. T. Suzuki and Shibayama Roshi. Over the decades, he came to the States each year to lecture, lead retreats, and give calligraphy demonstrations. Fukushima Roshi's lectures were rich and varied, moving fluidly from insights into Joshu's teaching and comments on "no mind" (*mushin*), to charming anecdotes about his everyday encounters, perspectives on religion, human relationships, the challenges facing the modern world, and more.

THE MOST IMPORTANT editorial question we faced in organizing this book was how to provide readers with the broadest, most coherent experience of Fukushima Roshi's teachings for Americans. To meet this objective, we've organized chapters according to the topics about which Fukushima Roshi spoke most often and with the greatest interest and depth, combining passages from different sources in each chapter. As a result of being edited for print, the looser and more playful feeling of his live teaching in lectures and conversation is a bit under-represented. Fukushima Roshi sometimes took off on tangents, talking about people he'd met in his travels or places he'd visited. He was very fond of chocolate and of bridges, and he mentioned them more often than these chapters might lead you to believe.

Fukushima Roshi spoke to us about the importance of *zenga*, the actual and exact Zen words and expressions of a Zen master. Our abiding goal has been to most closely preserve his zenga. We wanted the reader to hear Zen in his voice, and according to his wishes, we wanted to make his teachings available in English. Fukushima Roshi loved Americans, and one of his life goals was to help Americans understand authentic Rinzai Zen and develop an American way of Zen.

May it be so.

"Harmonizing with Difficult Circumstances"

Calligraphy by Keido Fukushima

I.

What Is Zen?

Stop and Look
Under Your Own Feet

Look at your own feet; examine yourself and what you
are doing.

IN ZEN WE SAY, "Look under your own feet" (*kyakka shoko*). These
are the words of Master Sanko Kokushi (1271–1361). He inscribed
this message near the bottom of a large pole at the entrance to the
kitchen at his temple. Because he wrote the message near the bottom
of the pole, visitors read it as a request that they arrange their shoes
neatly. But this is not the Zen meaning of the expression.

Nowadays, people don't arrange their shoes neatly because they
are not taught to do so within the family culture at home. So, in a
way, understanding "Look under your own feet" to be an encouragement to straighten your shoes is good. But the actual source of
the expression was a *mondo*—a public dialogue—between Sanko
Kokushi and a disciple.

The disciple asked him, "What is the meaning of Bodhidharma
coming to China from India?"

"Look under your own feet," Sanko Kokushi replied.

Bodhidharma carried Zen from India to China. So the disciple's question amounts to asking, "What is Zen?" Sanko Kokushi
answered with this one phrase: "Look under your own feet."

Newspapers sometimes invert the phrase so it reads *shoko kyakka*. But Sanko Kokushi expressed the true meaning, the correct phrase. A literal Japanese reading would be "the foot (*kyakka*) upon which the light shines (*shoko*)." The foot comes first, but not someone else's foot; it's your own foot! Consider your own actions! This is a teaching about self-examination, introspection. People neglect to examine themselves, to really look thoroughly at their own feet, to truly self-reflect. People tend to look at others and forget to examine themselves. Sanko Kokushi's teaching is about keenly looking at ourselves, with a steady gaze.

I was among the last generation to pass through the old Japanese system of education. At the end of World War II, I was receiving the last of that old-fashioned system. I experienced the bombing and then the rebuilding of Japan thereafter. When Japan lost the war, the economy bottomed out and everyone began to scramble to rebuild, including even those who were supposed to be guardians of the temples. As a result of all this scrambling, Japan's economic growth after the war has earned special mention in world history.

But now the force of our own momentum drives us to move too quickly, pushed by our habitual scrambling. When you rush, you forget things. You don't even notice when you drop something. We have forgotten one thing in the last fifty years of scrambling: our souls or hearts (*kokoro*). These last fifty years have brought material improvement, but we have not developed the life of the soul, the spiritual life. So now we Japanese people have a rich material life, but the Japanese heart, the Japanese soul, suffers from a kind of vacancy. This is the situation in which we find ourselves in Japan.

As a monk living in the modern world I believe that in order to really watch yourself you must first come to a stop. When you come to a stop you can then see the world. Coming to a stop and pausing, you can understand the world. We have an expression in Japanese that communicates the importance of taking time to notice: "Looking at a friend's back." Friends may not look so happy when you look at their backs. At such times, you may realize your own back is unhappy too. Such realization is only possible if we come to a stop. If you're in a rush and walking in the wrong direction, for example, you may go a long distance without noticing the mistake you are making. When you stop, you can realize your mistake and make the necessary correction.

Once a month I travel to Osaka by train to give a Zen lecture. If I arrive early, I get off the train at the shopping level of the station and watch the people of Osaka as they shop. They are a representative sample of modern-day Japanese people rushing around. Egotism sprouts like horns and shoppers resemble stampeding buffalos. This is not only the case in Osaka; it's the same in Nagoya, Kyoto, and especially Tokyo. The scramble and rush is characteristic of every big city in Japan, and people probably scramble the fastest in Tokyo.

I was standing by a pole in the station watching people and thinking about how they were rushing around. A high school student ran into me and said, "Watch where you're going, you shit monk!"

I stopped him and asked, "What did you say?"

The student lowered his head and replied, "I'm sorry I called you a shit monk."

I told him I didn't mind him calling me a shit monk: "If I am a shit monk, then you are a shit student. Everybody has shit. I don't mind that part. It's what you said before that. You said, 'Watch where you're going!' I was standing still and you bumped into me. It's you who needs to watch where you're going!"

If I had stopped a businessman who'd bumped into me and asked him the same question, he would've probably called me a "shit monk" again. Meeting the student was an unusual turn of events: he was young and innocent, and he apologized.

It takes courage to stop, but it doesn't mean you stay stopped. It's just a matter of stopping for a little while to take a good look at your feet and what's going on around you. In the middle of our struggle for existence we need the courage to stop, even if it's just for a little while. By mustering the courage to stop, you may find a meaningful next step or even a new direction.

Look at your own feet; examine yourself and what you are doing.

Dependent Co-origination
and Attachment

I shouldn't say this, but sometimes chocolates taste
so good they're even better than satori. . . . If I wanted
the chocolates so badly that I pushed others out of
the way to get them, that's not okay.

BUDDHISM BEGAN IN India with the enlightenment of the historical buddha, Shakyamuni. His enlightenment experience is really
the foundation of Buddhism. I began my college studies with the
study of Indian Buddhism, taking on the subject of the Buddha's
enlightenment in my first year. I'd like to explain in a few words what
it took me a whole year to learn about his enlightenment.

An essential aspect of the Buddha's enlightenment is called
dependent co-origination; this was a great discovery. Most of us
think that things exist independently. But a thing exists only because
of everything else that exists. If you don't understand this, you don't
understand Buddhism.

Take the *nioi*, for example. It is a small wooden stick that is a
symbol of a Zen master. It is a small stick only because there is
such a thing as a long stick. During Zen meditation a senior monk
carries a long stick called a *kyosaku*, literally "the wake-up stick."
If a monk falls asleep in meditation, the senior monk will hit him
with the long stick. I didn't bring a long stick to America. It seems

Americans aren't fond of being hit with long sticks; they seem frightened by it. Still some students overcame this problem and became my disciples.

I no longer bring long sticks to teach outside of Japan because they don't fit well with other cultures. But I do occasionally hit people with my small stick. In the monastery we do koan study. Sometimes monks come up with really stupid answers. It would be awkward to simply say "That doesn't make sense," so I hit them without any comment. But normally I don't use my small stick to hit people.

In any case, let's say that in the whole universe there is only this one short stick. Then we wouldn't need to call it a "short stick." We wouldn't even need to call it "this," because there would be no "that." But in the real universe there are short and long sticks; there is this and there is that. The reason this is a small stick is because cups of water, chairs, tables, and everything else exists. Similarly, let's say that you were the only thing that existed in the whole universe. If this were the case you wouldn't need a term to describe yourself. In reality, there are many people in the world. You exist as you and nobody else because of all the other people in the world who are not you. This is what the law of dependent co-origination is all about.

Thinking about things in this way, we can relax. But when we're thinking about ourselves, we prefer to think we're entirely unique and exist separately from others. Yet we exist only because of everything else in the universe. This applies not only to human relationships but to any relationship. When we say "self and other," we could even mean "me and this glass of water": me as self and glass of water as other.

Shakyamuni Buddha's notion of dependent co-origination isn't just a philosophical matter. Humans tend to be arrogant. In European philosophy we say, "I think therefore I am." This is okay. But Buddhism views matters from a different angle. European philosophy tends to think that first there's a self, and because of the self, the world comes to be.

But Buddhism teaches that because everything exists, the self comes to be. So when I say that I am here, I'm not just referring to a detached, unique self, separate from everything else; I exist because of everything else that exists. This is why in Buddhism we say that there's no intrinsic nature. The notion of no intrinsic nature is based on dependent co-origination and is called *shunyata* in Indian Buddhism. *Shunyata* is translated as "emptiness." Because everything exists interdependently with everything else, nothing has an intrinsic nature. Everything is empty. If we had to rely on just one word to express all of Buddhism, it would be emptiness. This is the most basic, essential teaching of Buddhism.

It's difficult to understand, isn't it? You can see that Indian Buddhism has a very philosophical bent, but Buddhism is a religion and all religions teach people how to live their lives. If we talk only about things like dependent co-origination and emptiness, it's difficult to find a way to live, but there's another essential concept in Buddhism called *muga*—a state of no-ego. The concept of no-ego is also rather philosophical. But compared to the teaching of dependent co-origination, no self-nature, and emptiness, the teaching of no-ego is more helpful in relation to how to live our lives. By realizing our own no-ego, we try to live a life free from selfishness.

In Buddhism we say humans have 108 different delusions. We're full of delusions. Our delusions can eat breakfast, lunch, and dinner. In fact there are so many delusions, we could assume that everything is a delusion—delusion is understood, in this context, to be the same as attachment. Actually though, in our everyday lives, some attachments are fine, like wanting to study. If we said the desire to study is an attachment and thus a delusion, nobody would go to university. The desire to study is an example of a good attachment. Or take the desire to make enough money to support yourself and your family. This is another kind of attachment that's fine. There are attachments that are good and attachments that are not. The attachment to study is a good attachment. I prefer to call it a desire, which is something natural. However if you want to do well in school to such an extent that you'll betray your closest friends, then you've gone too far and it's no longer a desire; it's become a delusion. Or in the case of money, if you want it so badly that you'll kill for it, it's a delusion.

So how do we distinguish between desires and delusions? We distinguish based on whether the ego's involved or not! Personally, I'm very fond of chocolate. It's quite delicious. I shouldn't say this, but sometimes chocolates taste so good they're even better than satori. I'm also quite fond of coffee. I don't drink alcohol, but I really like coffee. And I'm fond of bridges. My monks know that I'm fond of chocolate, coffee, and bridges. Once, one of the senior monks asked me jokingly if my fondness for chocolate, coffee, and bridges was a kind of attachment. As a Zen master I answered that such kinds of attachments are okay. The point is that some attachments are fine, and some attachments are not. The issue is whether your ego is involved. If I wanted the chocolates so badly that I pushed others out of the way to get them, that's not okay. The question is whether the ego's wrapped up in it or not. Buddhism talks of a life free from attachment; if you haven't realized this state of no-ego, you can't live such a life. This is the sense in which the teaching of no-ego is so important. This is where the realization of dependent co-origination actually shows up in your life—when you find that you, your ego, and everything you encounter are not independent. You are connected to everything.

3

Zen Is the Religion of Mu

With respect to the concept of Mu, there is an understanding that everything is nothing, that nothing is
everything. . . . If you try to grasp this concept through
the powers of the intellect, it's going to be very hard,
but if you try to comprehend it experientially, it's not
so hard.

ZEN IS THE RELIGION of *Mu*. My interpreter uses the term
Mu without translating it into English. This is because *Mu* really
shouldn't be translated. For a long time, I've considered English to
be the language of the world (although the French might not agree).
But not every word can or should be translated into English, especially when translation leads to misunderstanding. This goes for the
Zen word *Mu*.

When *Mu* is translated into English, it is taken to mean things like
"nothing" or "no being." Translating it as "nothing" makes it sound
very negative. But in Zen, Mu doesn't just have a negative meaning;
Mu doesn't just refer to nothing. Mu means although it is, it isn't, and
although it isn't, it is. This is why it's better to leave it untranslated.

With respect to the concept of Mu, there is an understanding
that everything is nothing, that nothing is everything. This is a basic
Buddhist notion and it is hard to grasp. Japanese students also find
it hard. If you try to grasp this concept through the powers of the

intellect, it's going to be very hard, but if you try to comprehend it experientially, it's not so hard. For a Zen master, it's easy to understand, but for most people, including the Japanese, this notion of Mu is hard to grasp. It's difficult for philosophers to understand as well.

There's a type of paper bag in Japan that has become quite popular recently. On the outside of the bag there are various designs or logos. Not too long ago, I saw one with the cartoon character Snoopy on it. It showed Snoopy surprised by something, falling backward, and coming out of his mouth as he fell was the word *mu*. I said, "Look at that. Even Snoopy knows about Mu." Right now in my monastery in Japan, there are fifteen monks training under me, and Mu is the first koan given to them. The Mu koan is difficult. There are 102 subquestions within it. If a monk gives it his all, he can get through all of them in about three years. After about a year, when he hasn't been able to get through it, he may start coming up with stupid answers. So to encourage the monk at that point, I sometimes say, "You don't understand it? Even Snoopy can understand it!"

In the world of philosophy and in the world of common sense, when something exists, it exists, and when something doesn't, it doesn't. That's the common-sense view. What makes the notion of Mu so difficult is that while everything exists, nothing exists, and while nothing exists, everything exists. Because of this profound meaning of Mu, we can't simply translate it as "nothing." In addition translating Mu as "nothing" creates a very negative impression, but the Mu of Zen includes both the affirmative and the negative. It is essential to understand this if you want to understand Zen.

If you don't comprehend this notion—that while everything exists, nothing exists, and while nothing exists, everything exists— it's difficult to understand Buddhism, including Zen Buddhism. There are about three thousand sutras, or Buddhist sacred scriptures. The Prajnaparamita, or Perfection of Wisdom, sutras are one set of these sutras, made up of six hundred volumes. The essence of all these volumes is expressed in the *Heart Sutra*, and the central phrase in the *Heart Sutra* is while everything exists, nothing exists, while nothing exists, everything exists.

Philosophers have a tough time with this notion. When I was at university, my professor told me about a conversation between D. T. Suzuki and the philosopher Martin Heidegger. Heidegger asked Suzuki over and over again, "What is Zen? What is Zen?" D. T. Suzuki was quite proficient in English and gave Heidegger the same answer over and over again. I'm sure when Heidegger kept hearing that while everything exists, nothing exists, and while nothing exists, everything exists, such an answer was difficult for him to accept. At first he must have thought Zen was pretty screwed up. But Heidegger, being as intelligent as he was, finally understood. Finally he said, "Ah! So that's what Zen teaches." And at this D. T. Suzuki pounded his fist on the table and said, "That's what I've been saying all along!"

Still, Heidegger's understanding was purely intellectual, and when we talk about Mu in Zen it's not just a concept, it's a living experience. In the world of logic and reason, it makes no sense that something exists and doesn't exist, and at the same time it doesn't exist and it exists. But this is something you can actually experience. And this experience is an individual matter. It's the experience where you yourself become Mu.

What does it mean to become Mu? It means to completely cut off and eliminate your egoistic side. If you do Zen training, as you proceed, you cut off more and more of your egoistic side, and at the same time, you become more and more Mu and you feel you're being reborn. In this way, you can actually experience that while everything is, nothing is, and while nothing is, everything is.

Conversion is a Christian term, but I refer to this experience of becoming Mu as a religious conversion. As you cut off more and more of your egoistic side and become Mu, a new self is born. We call this the self of *mushin*, the self of empty mind. We say Zen is the religion of satori, the religion of enlightenment. Zen satori is to realize the self of empty mind, of mushin.

Mushin is sometimes translated as "no mind." D. T. Suzuki usually translated *mushin* in this way. But this leads to misunderstanding. Chinese and Japanese Zen prefers concrete expression, but I also use the term "transcending dualism" to talk about becoming Mu. I'm aware that I'm using philosophical terminology from D. T. Suzuki. Indian Buddhism was philosophical. Chinese Buddhism was concrete. Japanese Buddhism continued with this concreteness. After World War II D. T. Suzuki wanted to bring Zen to the West where people were more intellectual, so he felt concreteness wasn't the best way to introduce Zen. He reverted to something closer to the philosophical style of Indian Buddhism and invented the term "transcending dualism." D. T. Suzuki was a great scholar and, as a monk, he underwent severe Zen training, so he was able to teach from experience as well. He used the term "transcending dualism" because he thought it suited Westerners and it turned out to be quite successful.

But as with Mu, I think it's better not to translate *mushin* at all, because it has so many meanings. When we translate it as "no mind," we risk imagining that it means "no thinking." The term *-shin*, or *mind*, in *mushin* is difficult to translate because it has many different facets.

If I ask Westerners where their mind is, they point to their heads. That's because people believe the mind equals thinking. But in Japanese, the term *shin* has many different parts; mind, heart, spirit, and sometimes even soul are all wrapped up in this one word. If one asks Asians where their mind is, instead of pointing to their heads, most would point to their stomachs, or some to their chests.

I always say, "My mind is very great." In part I say this in a joking way, but I'm serious. It is a joke because I have a fat stomach. But it is also a serious statement, because the mind must be great. It must be wide. It must be open. In Europe they translate *mushin* as "empty mind." When Prince Charles came to Tofukuji for a visit five years ago, he used the term "empty mind." Between the two translations— "no mind" and "empty mind"—perhaps "empty mind" is a little bit better.

Because the mind is empty, it can freely respond to anything. Because the mind is empty it can freely take in anything. Empty mind is also free mind. Think about yourself with a mind free to adapt and able to take in anything. There is a very fresh feeling to such a mind, and so empty mind is also fresh mind. And because one takes in everything afresh, one is also able to create, so empty mind is also creative mind.

Thus the "no mind" of mushin is not "no thinking." Rather, it is thinking freely. If you believe that "no mind" means no thinking, this is actually a dead mind, a static mind. The free, fresh, creative mind is actually very dynamic. Zen Buddhism hates the static. Zen is not a dead religion. It is a living, working, dynamic religion. So mushin includes empty mind, free mind, fresh mind, creative mind, and pure mind. All these notions are included in mushin and the goal of Zen practice is to become this self of empty mind.

When you realize this self, you can live a life free of attachment. This is a life of freedom, the living enlightenment of Zen. And when you do become enlightened, it's not the end of it all. After your enlightenment, you must continue to deepen the experience. You may have an experience of satori, but as you deepen the experience, it becomes living enlightenment.

4

Zen and Prejudice

Zen hates discrimination and prejudice; all people
are buddhas.

Two monks came to visit Zen Master Joshu (778–897). Master
Joshu asked one of them if he'd visited the temple before, and the
monk replied that it was his first visit. Joshu offered him a cup of tea.
Today wherever you go in China, they will serve you tea and they'll
tell you their local tea is the best in all of China. But actually the town
of Joshu was quite famous for its excellent tea, and even today, they'll
serve you great tea at his temple.

After offering the first monk tea, Master Joshu turned to the other
monk and asked the same question: "Have you been here before?"
The other monk said he had been to the temple before. "Well then,
have a cup of tea," Joshu replied. Joshu's head monk was standing
nearby and thought this was quite strange. He said to the master, "I
understand why you offered tea to the monk who was visiting for the
first time, but I don't understand why you also had tea served to the
monk who'd been here before."

This was the head monk's question: Why offer tea to both monks?

Master Joshu addressed the head monk by his title, calling out,
"Head monk!"

The head monk replied, "Yes, Master."

"Have some tea."

This story illustrates a Zen teaching of action in a state of empty mind. Zen begins and ends with empty mind. In Zen this state of mind is both empty and free. In every moment we creatively adapt, with freshness. Empty mind is at once empty, free, creative, and fresh. We also use the term "pure mind" to refer to this state of mind.

You may understand this intellectually, but you aren't living a Zen life unless you live every day in this state. Old Master Joshu lived in this state of empty mind. Whoever comes—the first monk, the second monk, or his attendant—Joshu offers tea. This is acting in empty mind. Master Joshu is simply acting in and from this empty mind. For him there are no differences; he would offer tea to a man, to a woman, to someone who hadn't been there before, and to someone who had. But the head monk had not attained the state of empty mind, so he did not understand. He thought there was a difference between a first-time visitor and someone who'd been there before.

Zen hates discrimination and prejudice; all people are buddhas. The *Nirvana Sutra* teaches as its main point that all beings have buddha nature as their basic nature. All people have this buddha nature and, as buddhas, we are all equal. There is definitely a difference between lay life and monastic life, but the realization of no-ego is the same in both cases. This reflects an important aspect of Buddhist history. In the *Nirvana Sutra* the Buddha said, "All beings have buddha nature as their basic nature." This means that not just monks and nuns but all people, including laypeople, have this buddha nature.

However, historically in the Northern and Southern Schools of Chinese Buddhism, monastic life was emphasized and laypeople were secondary. This distinction conflicts with Shakyamuni Buddha's teaching. Nevertheless, in China and Korea the historical focus was on monastic life. That focus shifted a bit when Buddhism came to Japan. Nowadays in Japan, with the exception of some Zen masters, every Buddhist priest can marry and live a life similar to laypeople. It was only when Chinese forms of Buddhism came to Japan that laypeople came to occupy the primary position. It's ideal for a Buddhist priest to marry in Japan. But the situation is still not perfect, as nuns cannot yet marry.

Some buddhas are men and some buddhas are women. In America, Zen has been a religion primarily of lay practitioners since its inception. As a result of this the balance of male and female practitioners in America is about even. Consequently, in Japan there are many male Zen masters but few female masters, and in the United States the numbers are about equal. This is something unique to American Zen. One of the most important developments in American Zen is the equality of female Zen masters. From this perspective American Zen has come that much closer to Shakyamuni Buddha's ideal.

Some American Zen practitioners shave their heads, wear robes, and become monks or nuns. If they really want to do that, it's fine. But they shouldn't make such a decision just because they want to imitate the appearance of a monk or a monastic lifestyle. It's fine if a Zen master wears blue jeans! That's also unique about American Zen; there are many styles.

Zen recognizes that there are differences in the world, but it also recognizes equality. When people become attached to differences, they struggle to maintain equality. Zen hates anything prejudicial and teaches the transcendence of dualistic discrimination. In Zen we learn to respond with freedom to both sides of any duality.

No matter who comes, serve them tea. If you greet people, greet everyone.

5

Zen and Compassion

Transcending dualism doesn't mean doing away with dualistic discrimination. It means doing away with right and wrong from a self-centered perspective.

ALL BUDDHISM, including Zen, leads practitioners to enter the world with great compassion. To become a priest without any social sense is not good. Zen is not separate from society; Zen is concrete and based in daily life. All great religions ask us to live with great compassion. It's quite natural and good for Zen practitioners to oppose war and meet social problems with compassion. Monks eventually come to understand this as a result of their training. After constantly stripping away your own egotism you develop compassion for others. It arises naturally. Those who sincerely engage in training develop in such a way.

In Seoul there was a big conflict over who would be the successor to a large temple. Monks were fighting with each other. Monks and nuns should never fight. This happened because they didn't truly realize no-ego. Of course, in the real world we sometimes have conflict. If we've attained a state of no-ego, we can see clearly what's right and what's wrong, but if we're egotistical, we think of right and wrong in terms of our own self-centeredness. We can see without prejudice with no-ego. When two groups have a fight, we should say which is right and which is wrong. Transcending dualism doesn't mean doing away with dualistic discrimination. It means doing away with right and wrong from a self-centered perspective. Instead, we see the duality, we see both sides, and from our own free mind perspective we are able to freely adapt to both sides.

There is sunny weather and rainy weather. Transcending dualism doesn't do away with rainy days. Instead you dress appropriately for warm weather and take an umbrella when it rains. Sometimes it's warm, then it's cold, and then it's raining. Sometimes people complain about the weather, but I don't think anything of it. Zen is a religion that teaches us how we should live appropriately, here and now, just as ourselves. When the weather's cold we should respond to the cold. If it's cold I should wear a scarf. And when it rains, here and now, I should bring an umbrella.

Transcending dualism means to adapt within discrimination and dualism, to see both sides. Zen teaches this kind of transcendence, and this teaching includes freedom from attachments. When there's conflict you treat good as good and bad as bad. If one side is doing good, encourage them. If there's a group doing the wrong thing, tell them to stop. But adapting to these situations with true freedom— not from a self-centered view—this is practicing empty mind instead of indulging the ego.

The path to attaining no-ego is the religious person's path. Dealing with conflict before attaining no-ego is difficult because we put ourselves first, we see conflict subjectively in terms of our own situation, our own interests. If our egos are active, something that's essentially bad may feel to us as if it's good, because we have a self-centered perspective. Colorful flowers, for example, belong to the dualistic world. There are white flowers and red flowers. We should see the white flowers as white and red flowers as red. The distinction is clear in the case of flowers. But in complex situations things that are clearly black, clearly bad, may appear to be white and good, due to the influence of ego. We may even say that something good is bad.

Of course there are Zen priests who go through the training yet remain egotistical. When a monk is still in the monastery, the master can see his egotism, warn the monk, and work with him on it. But there are those cases where, without doing away with his ego, a monk leaves the monastery to assume the role of the lone priest of a small temple. One monk I know was like this. He trained for a very long time but still had a very strong ego. We once held a meeting of thirty priests at the monastery. As head abbot I sat in the uppermost seat. The priests were arranged by age; if two priests were the same age, they were seated according to years of training. The priest in question arrived late. If he'd been on time, he would have been just three seats away from me. But since he arrived late, he took the furthest seat. At first he said nothing. Then we had a meal and a little sake. Finally, he stood up in front of everyone and angrily complained about having to sit in the furthest seat. The other priests scolded him, saying that all his time in the monastery hadn't gotten rid of one iota of his egotism. He's actually a good temple priest, but he has a very strong ego. One of the other priests at the meeting told me how upset they all were that their colleague was so self-centered and suggested that as head abbot I should say something to him. I refused. I said that it wouldn't help; until he realized for himself what a strong ego he had, there was no point in me saying anything about it. There was nothing to be done. I said we would just have to wait until he died. Such cases occur when a monk doesn't get adequate training under a good master.

The same stubborn egotism applies in lay life. I will tell you a story about an old lady who lives near my monastery. She has come to every public meditation session and has attended many of my lectures since I became Zen master there. I sometimes run into her in the neighborhood. At one such encounter she told me about a woman living across the street from her who didn't like her and had never greeted her. "You've been listening to these lectures for a long time," I advised her, "Enter a state of empty mind. You must be able to greet anyone, including this woman across the street." The old lady said she'd tried saying hello but got no response. She said that when the woman left her house across the street in the morning, she would always look away so that it was really impossible to greet her. I slapped her on the back and said, "You just have to do it!"

The next day she phoned to say that she'd done it. "It's been twenty years since I said hello to the lady across the street. I saw her this morning and said 'Good morning' in a loud voice. She was so happy her face lit up and she said good morning right back!" This is what the old lady told me over the phone.

Of course, the woman across the street had really been a perfectly good person all along. But the old lady had been stuck with her own prejudice. Empty mind is a good way to work on prejudice and selfishness in everyday life and to discover compassion.

6

Zen Is a Matter of Awareness

Whether we are Buddhist or Christian, we must keep in mind that religion is a matter of awareness, of awakening to something.

WE COULD CALL ZEN "the religion of the self" or "the self of Mu." In other words, we can say that Zen is realizing one's own no-ego for oneself.

Imagine a lit candle with a flame. Let's say you put your finger into the flame. I don't think anyone would be so stupid as to think that, because it's Sunday or a holiday, their finger wouldn't be burned. When you put your finger into a flame, even without intending to, you immediately pull it away. There is no ego at that moment. It's not that there is nothing whatsoever. It's just that there's only the experience of pain in that moment. In Zen we call this "pure experience." If you realize no-ego with that pure experience, that's the satori enlightenment of Zen.

You may think that pure experience sounds like some kind of regression to primitive instincts, but I'm speaking about something different. It's *realizing* no-ego in the experience. We could say that an infant lives purely in that world, but the infant isn't aware of it, she doesn't realize it. That's the difference. Whether we are Buddhist or Christian, we must keep in mind that religion is a matter of awareness, of awakening to something. Our tendency to analyze everything intellectually makes it difficult to remember this.

I once used the above example of the flame with a professor I know. At the time he was very deeply studying Hegelian philosophy so his mind was filled with philosophical ideas and analyses. The day after I explained the flame analogy to him, he responded with two full pages of questions and comments on it. It was quite an undertaking to read through his response, given my limited ability with English, but using a dictionary, I managed to get through it. It turns out that he didn't understand my example of the flame. The way he understood it, there must first be a subjective self, then there must be an objective flame in relation with the subject. Then the subject must act to move toward the object, at which point the sense of heat could be transmitted to the subject. His explanation was logical and analytical, but it completely missed the point of Zen pure experience. The point is that there is no ego at the actual moment of feeling the heat. This is called the self of Mu. And this self of Mu is the subject—buddha nature.

Let me illustrate this with a few more examples. Around the time that Joshu lived, there was a Zen master named Gutei. Throughout his teaching life all he did to express buddha nature was to raise one finger. This was his creative way of expressing his own buddha nature. He never responded with words, but just with one finger. If someone asked him, "What is buddha nature?" he would simply raise one finger. In this way, he showed that he himself was completely buddha nature. This is well known as "Gutei's One-Finger Zen." But if we don't see how Gutei was demonstrating his own buddha nature, the story has no meaning. Gutei's One-Finger Zen expresses the substantial form of buddha nature. When what one does or says expresses one's buddha nature, anything is okay.

Zen Master Zuigan provides another example. Master Zuigan was a somewhat peculiar individual. We Zen monks understand him, even though he seems a bit strange to the average person. Zuigan would sit in zazen in his temple and would call out to himself. He'd say, "Master," to which he would respond, "Yes?" He'd say, "Are you fully awake?" to which he'd answer, "Yes, I am." He'd then say, "From now on, don't be fooled by anything others say," to which he would answer, "I understand." He would have this conversation with himself as he sat in zazen. Zuigan used the term *master* to express his own buddha nature. If the one who called out "Master!" had already realized this buddha nature, Zuigan's buddha nature, then the Zuigan who answered "Yes?" also has Zuigan's buddha nature. If you do not understand it in this light, you cannot understand it as a Zen story. This is how Zuigan expressed his buddha nature.

Finally, we find an example in a story about Zen Master Joshu. A monk came to Joshu and asked, "What is the Buddha?" This is the same as asking "What is buddha nature?" or "What is your true nature?" There were many great oak trees in front of Joshu's temple in China. Today only seven remain. In fact, Joshu's temple was called Oak Tree Temple due to the number of oaks around it. When the monk asked Joshu, "What is the Buddha?" Joshu answered, "An oak tree." He was able to express himself freely. This oak tree story is quite famous.

The exact translation of his reply is: "An oak tree in the garden before me." The great Japanese Zen scholar D. T. Suzuki translated it as "The oak tree in the garden." Sometimes it's mistakenly translated as "The oak tree in the front garden." The important thing to realize, as Suzuki did, is that it is an oak tree in the garden *before* me. He realized this and so didn't use the term "in the front garden." The Chinese text includes the character for *front*. The actual meaning of this character for *front* is "in front of me." That's why I translate it as

"An oak tree in the garden before me." Since the old Chinese doesn't use plural forms, we can't tell if Joshu was talking about one oak tree or many oak trees. When I saw Suzuki's translation, I thought that Joshu must have meant only one oak tree. It's okay that there's only one oak tree, because if you yourself do not become one with this one oak tree, you can never show your own true buddha nature.

When you perfect your Zen state of mind, your awareness becomes quite free. A monk came to Joshu and Joshu asked him where he came from. The monk answered, "I come from no direction." This is a good answer. When someone asks where you come from, you usually say "Japan" or "New York." But the monk gave Joshu a very good answer. He was a good monk. When monks give such answers, they must bow deeply to the master. The monk gave his answer and began to bow deeply to Joshu. But Joshu turned around. What was the monk to do? He was now bowing to Joshu's backside! The monk scrambled around to the other side, and now facing Joshu, bowed deeply. Truly he came from no direction. In other words, he had no attachment to direction.

Many Chinese temples have a second floor; this monk would have chased Joshu to the second floor and bowed deeply. What if Joshu had gone to the toilet? I'm sure the monk would have gone in with him. No direction. Zen Master Joshu turned around, so the monk scrambled around to face him. Zen Master Joshu praised the monk. Of the 525 stories in the *Record of Joshu*, there are only about fifty in which Joshu praises a monk. How did he praise the monk? He said to the monk, "Your 'no direction' is grand."

7

Living and Dying Fully

After living this life to its fullest, the moment death
arrives, we can die to its fullest.

This is what Zen teaches about being human.

AFTER D. T. SUZUKI turned eighty, he spent most of his time
at Columbia University in New York. A Mr. S. was taking care of
Professor Suzuki at that time. Mr. S. frequently attended Suzuki's
lectures and read all his books; he had developed a deep understanding of Zen. Years later, Mr. S. visited my monastery, Tofukuji, and
told me a story that had not been written down anywhere.

One morning he and Professor Suzuki were eating breakfast
together and Mr. S. asked, "What is Zen, really?" Professor Suzuki
said nothing for a while. Then he slapped himself on the leg. Mr.
S. nodded. Three days passed and again they were having breakfast. Professor Suzuki asked Mr. S., "Three days ago when I slapped
myself on the thigh, you nodded. What is it that you understood?"
Mr. S. answered, "Zen is here and now." That was the correct answer.
Professor Suzuki said, "If you understand that, that's great. What
Zen is teaching is here, now, and ourselves!"

In Japanese, we say *"ima, koko,"* or "now and here." In English, the
expression is "here and now." Whether *now* or *here* comes first, Zen
teaches that this very moment is of the utmost importance. In this very

moment I'm talking to you and you are listening and that's what our lives are about, living in this moment. So when you eat, concentrate on eating. And when you walk, walk. This is the basis of Zen teaching. Understand that what's important is to live our lives every day.

Here and now also means understanding that someday we're going to die. Every year I travel by car and plane. The head monk in my monastery comes with me, leaving the second and third most senior head monks to take care of the monastery in my absence. Before I left one of them asked me how many plane flights I'd be taking this time. I told him about eighteen. The monk said this year I was going to crash. He said this as a joke, but I've been thinking it could be true. Sometime during my travels my plane might crash. If that happens and the plane goes into a dive, everyone will likely panic. I was thinking to myself, if it did come to that, I'd like to give my last sermon to the panicking people on the plane. But I haven't written a manuscript yet for that sermon.

We can't know when and how death will come. It's something for which we can't really prepare. We can make a hotel reservation, but we can't make a reservation for death. The emphasis in Zen is on us ourselves, here and now. We need to know life is not only happiness. Sometimes life is pain. We can meet both experiences with the same attention if we receive the happy days with appreciation and we live with strength on the painful days. This practice is a way of life: applying ourselves equally—with equal strength—to both happy days and painful days. This is our fine life.

The great Japanese poet Ryokan wrote:

When a painful day is met,
the painful day is met with welcome;
at the time of death,
death is met with welcome.

WE HAVE TO meet painful days naturally and freely. There is no choice but to meet the pain. The pain, the painful day, cannot go anywhere else. People usually think that enjoyment depends on good circumstances. Ryokan's poem turns our usual idea of enjoying life completely on its head, so that we understand to enjoy painful days and enjoy death. To meet everything—sunny days and rainy days— equally is to understand how to meet and enjoy a painful day.

This life is not continuous happiness. When we meet with painful times, going all the way to the bottom of unhappiness, we need to know how to react to such difficulties. In order to live fully, we must understand how we can live in painful situations. The secret is to apply ourselves equally in every situation. This means that we need to do our best in life. When we think about it, death is the end of the line. Ninety-nine-point-nine percent of your life occurs before this point of death, so we can see that the whole effort is about living. Living means applying ourselves completely to happiness and applying ourselves completely to unhappiness. And this ability to apply ourselves regardless of circumstances is freedom.

We can't anticipate the time of our death. We don't get to make a reservation for our death like we do for a seat on the bullet train. Death can happen suddenly. So if we keep trying our best in life, responding freely to happiness and unhappiness, then when death comes, we will also do our best. This is the Mahayana way of realization in everyday life. This is what Zen Master Ummon meant when he said, "Every day is a fine day." It is really a teaching about freedom in everyday life.

The important thing is to be concerned about living. There's really no need to be concerned about death. Just live life to its fullest up to the very moment of death. Every religion, including Buddhism, teaches about death. But the most important teaching is about how to live. This is how Zen sees the human condition: To live every moment to its fullest, moment by moment. Moment by moment we live one day. Then another day, and then, day by day, we live a year. And in this way a whole life is lived. After living this life to its fullest, the moment death arrives, we can die to its fullest.

This is what Zen teaches about being human.

8

Everyday Mind Is the Way

Many people have this same kind of misunderstanding, imagining that Zen practice arouses supernatural powers and you become Superman. If I do become Superman through Zen practice, I will be sure to start wearing a cape and fly around to Wagnerian music.

WHEN JOSHU WAS in his thirties, he asked Master Nansen, "What is the Way?" Nansen answered, "Everyday mind itself is the Way," whereupon Joshu had his first enlightenment experience. This was an important teaching of Nansen's. When we talk about the Way of Zen, that Way isn't somewhere special. It's in each of us in our everyday minds. Many people think Zen is something special, something *out there*. Some people even think that you develop special or supernatural powers by practicing Zen.

I lived in an institute in the graduate school of Claremont College in Southern California for a year. A friend invited me to come with her to visit someone in a hospital located out in the desert. I went with her and brought an Indian scholar friend along. The desert was quite beautiful. My Indian friend and I were waiting in the hospital lobby when an American gentleman approached me. Seeing my shaved head and black robe, he asked if I was a Zen monk. I answered that I was. He then asked me if I could do judo, to which I said no. I told him I watch judo on TV but can't do it. Next, he asked if I knew karate. No. "How about wrestling?" he asked. Again, I said no. How about sumo? Once again I had to answer no. He finally asked, "Then what can you do?" I said, "Sitting meditation." He replied, "Well then, you're not such a great Zen monk after all."

He did not understand Zen. A Zen monk does Zen practice. The man in the lobby had the idea that practicing Zen somehow makes you able to do anything. Personally, I don't do much at all besides Zen practice. In Japan many people have this same kind of misunderstanding, imagining that Zen practice arouses supernatural powers and you become Superman. If I do become Superman through Zen practice, I will be sure to start wearing a cape and fly around to Wagnerian music. My point is that when we say the Way is found in everyday life itself, we mean it really is right here, not somewhere far away.

Once, a monk asked Chosa, another of Nansen's disciples, "Your master always talks about everyday mind, but what does it really mean?" Chosa answered, "When you're tired, sleep. When you go to meditate, meditate." But these examples were too down to earth for the monk and he persisted, "I don't understand, please explain." Chosa answered, "When it's hot, cool down. When it's cold, wear something warm." Today we would say, "In the summer, turn on the A/C. In the winter, turn on the heater."

There's nothing far out or special about Zen at all. The mind in everyday life is life itself. But this idea is hard to grasp if you believe Zen is somewhere special. However, the Way of Zen is not special at all; everything in daily life is the Way of Zen. This is Zen's essential teaching about how to live, this teaching of everyday mind.

But this does raise a question: Since everyone is living an everyday life—why isn't everybody enlightened? How is it that this everyday life can lead to enlightenment? The Third Patriarch of Zen said something important regarding this question: "The way of enlightenment is not difficult, all you have to do is get rid of the discriminating mind that decides one thing is good and another is bad." Just get beyond this way of thinking and everyday mind is actually the way of enlightenment. This is the Zen teaching of the transcendence of dualism.

D. T. Suzuki first used the expression "to transcend dualism" when he introduced Zen to the West. He believed Westerners were more intellectually inclined. But these are not the kinds of words the ancient Zen masters used. They didn't favor philosophical or pedantic language. Their way of expressing the transcendence of dualism was concrete. "If you scoop up water in your hands, the image of the moon can be seen in your hands. If you hold a flower in your hands, its fragrance will permeate your clothing." This is how the ancient masters expressed the transcendence of dualism.

Normally there is a dualistic opposition between you and the moon. It's you watching the moon as subject, and the moon being watched as object. But when you scoop up water so the moon appears in your own hands, you've become one with the moon. This is the state of transcendence of dualism. When you look at a flower, it's you looking at the flower and the flower being looked at. But the moment you say to yourself, "The fragrance of the beautiful flower permeates me," the limitations of dualism disappear. Such is the down-to-earth way of teaching based on ordinary life experience offered by ancient Chinese and Japanese Zen masters.

Even though Zen teaches us to live transcending dualism, our world, the real world, is full of dualistic opposites. There are mountains and rivers. There's hot and cold. There's red and white. There's pain and pleasure. There's good and bad. There's existence and nonexistence. There's self and other, and life and death. Everything exists in dualistic opposition. The world around us is completely filled with duality. So when I talk about transcending dualism, I'm not talking about a world other than this one. You can ride in a spaceship to the end of the universe and never find a place free from dualistic opposition. In teaching about the transcendence of dualism, Zen does not deny this real world.

When we say ordinary mind and everyday life are the Way, we are describing the actual experience of transcending dualism. We are not relying on the concept of transcending dualism. After having the actual experience, you can live your life freely in this world of dualistic oppositions. So how does one actually go about having the experience of transcending dualism? This is difficult for modern people because they are so intellectually inclined, and the intellect functions in the realm of dualism. So in Zen we say you first have to rid yourself of the control and domination of the intellect. This doesn't mean that Zen denies the intellect. But when you're actually engaged in Zen practice, if you don't first put your intellect out of the way, you won't be able to have an experience of transcending dualism.

The first aim in Zen training is for the self to become Mu, to become empty of intellect and concepts. By becoming Mu, or empty, the conceptual distinction between self and other disappears. This experience of becoming Mu is the actual experience of transcending dualism. What happens to our minds when we become Mu? We realize empty mind, and by realizing empty mind in our daily lives, we enter a life beyond the control of intellect, concepts, and ego. When we are able to become Mu (and we do this over and over again), we can truly say that everyday mind, our own mind of everyday life, has become the Way of Zen.

9

Zazen Instructions

In Zen we teach that when you sit, you should feel
that your back becomes a pillar between heaven and
earth.

IN ORDER TO DO ZAZEN, it's good to well establish a firm sitting
position. You must neatly arrange your body and your mind. Remove
your shoes and place them in neat order. Please take off your socks;
you will need to breathe through your feet. When you take off your
socks, don't just toss them anywhere; place them with care. When
you sit, try to arrange nice, neat, orderly lines, vertically and hori-
zontally. As a primary rule there should be no talking when doing
zazen.

I will explain the posture for zazen. It is good to get your hips
nice and high. If you don't do this, it will be hard on your back later.
You can use two blankets or a blanket and a cushion to elevate your
hips. But if the cushions are too far up under your legs, that will also
make it difficult to sit. I'll begin by explaining the full lotus posture,
but this doesn't necessarily mean that you have to sit like that from
the start.

To assume the full lotus, first place your right leg up on your left
thigh. The left leg is then pulled up to rest on the right thigh. This
is the proper full lotus position. If you can't get both legs up, it is
acceptable to place only one leg up in what's known as a half lotus.

You can use either leg in the half lotus, whichever is more comfortable for you. No matter which leg you use, it is important to try to get your knees to touch the ground. This is why it's really easier to sit in full lotus: it sets both knees firmly on the floor. In half lotus one knee will tend to move and wobble. If you can't get your knee down, place your bottom foot under the hanging knee. This may be a little difficult for Americans to do at first, so if your knees tend to stick out place a pillow underneath. If you don't do this to stabilize your posture while sitting, your legs will shudder.

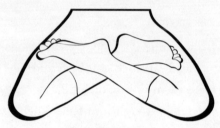

Full lotus posture

No matter which position you use, make sure your legs are comfortable in the position. In Japan many people make a mistake regarding this point, thinking that you can only do zazen in the full lotus position. While it is best to sit in full lotus, there are many cases in which it is impossible to sit in full lotus or even half lotus. Place your legs in a way that's comfortable for you as you sit. The idea that you can't do zazen if you can't do full lotus is wrong. It seems reasonable to think that you may not be able to do zazen if you have no legs at all, but actually, you could still do zazen even without legs! No matter what position your legs are in, you can still do zazen. Just do what's comfortable for you.

Next, straighten your back as much as you can. This is most important. The inability to straighten your back is an even bigger handicap than the position of your legs can be. Of course there are those whose backs may be bent because they are handicapped or disabled, or because they are elderly. But even people with bent backs or other impairments can do zazen. Both Americans and Japanese tend to slouch. Americans study bent over like this, and Japanese count money bent over like this. In general, it's good to straighten our backs to the best of our ability, so please straighten your back up as much as possible.

In Zen we teach that when you sit, you should feel that your back becomes a pillar between heaven and earth. After a long period of training with this thought in mind, Japanese monks do feel like their backs are a pillar between heaven and earth. If, as a layperson, you sit diligently for two years, you can develop this same feeling. Having a straight back is the most important part of zazen posture. In addition, do not hold any kind of power or tension in your shoulders. Flex your shoulders and let the tension out.

Alternate kneeling position, using a seiza bench or cushion

Basic zazen posture

Place your right hand naturally, palm up on top of your crossed legs. Let all of your fingers rest one against the other, without splaying them out. Place your left hand, palm up, squarely on top of the right. Let the fingers of the left hand rest on top of the fingers of the right, and touch the tips of the thumbs together, such that the placement of the hands and thumbs form an oval. Since the position of the legs will be different from person to person, where the hands come to rest on the legs will differ as well. If you hold your hands up too high, your shoulders will grow tight and tired, and if you place your hands too far forward, your whole body will lean forward and you'll start to fall over. So press your hands slightly against the lower part of your abdomen.

Hand placement

Once you have straightened your back and positioned your arms, straighten your neck and head. It should feel as if your head has been placed squarely atop your backbone. Pull your chin in just a little bit, but not too much. Close your mouth and breathe only through your nose. If you try to breathe through your mouth, you'll make a lot of noise. If you have a cold or nasal inflammation and can't breathe through your nose, it is okay to open your mouth a bit and breathe like that. The normal rule is to breathe through the nose with the mouth closed.

Leave your eyes in a half-opened position. But don't worry overmuch about whether your eyes are half open or not. First, simply close your eyes, then open them a little. You can see with your eyes half open, so where should you focus your sight? The line of sight should typically be to a point about three feet in front of you. Your eyes will naturally settle at that distance. But this is only a basic rule, and since the natural gaze of the eyes will differ from person to person, it's okay if your eyes rest on a point a little closer or a little further away. However, if you look at a point too close to you, your head will begin to droop, and if you look at a point too far away from you, your head will begin to rise. This is why the focal point should ideally be about three feet in front of you.

Zazen breathing should be deep and quiet. But don't worry too much about trying to breathe deeply at the beginning. If you try to breathe deeply from the start, your breath will become constricted, and that's not the way to breathe in zazen. Begin with quiet, shallow breathing, and your breath will naturally begin to deepen. Then try to count breaths. When you exhale an in-breath, count one. Count inside your own head. When you inhale and exhale again, count two. Do it again and that's three. When you get to ten, throw out the numbers and go back to one.

"Practice ten years,
then ten more years,
then ten more years."

Calligraphy by Keido Fukushima

II.

My Zen Training

My First Training Master

*My master made a big effort to train us and he
wanted us to concentrate on whatever we were doing
in the moment.*

MY FIRST MASTER was quite funny. I have many memories of
him. In junior high I had a chemistry test. There were four older
disciples at the temple and every day we had different temple work to
do, and on the day before the test it was my job to heat water for the
bath. When the water was hot enough, I went to my teacher's room
to tell him the bath was ready. Nowadays many visitors stay at my
home temple, but at that time only my teacher and his five disciples
lived at the temple. It was quiet and our teacher concentrated on our
education as monks.

When my teacher thought it was nearing time for a bath, he'd set
his towels on the table and wait. When I came to tell him the bath
was ready, he'd get right up and go directly to the bath. The bath in a
Japanese temple is not like a Western bath; it's some distance from
the main temple building. In the case of our temple it was a two- or
three-minute walk. On this particular occasion, when I went to tell
my teacher that the bath was ready, he didn't come right out in his
usual manner. He may have been on the phone or something; I don't
know. So I returned to my position heating the bath and resumed
studying my chemistry book.

Zen monks are trained to walk silently, so when my master finally did come to the bath, he approached very quietly. Suddenly I noticed him standing right next to me. He asked what I was reading, and I told him I was reading my chemistry text. My master made a big effort to train us and he wanted us to concentrate on whatever we were doing in the moment. This meant I should have been concentrating on the bath. He told me I shouldn't be reading while doing my job at the bath. I told him without hesitation that I had a chemistry test the next day. Even now I still marvel at how angry my master could get, but he didn't get angry. He said, "So you have a test tomorrow, do you? Okay, I'll give you a chemistry problem." You know, Zen masters aren't necessarily chemistry experts.

Here's the problem he gave me: "You have three kinds of white powder—one is sugar, one is salt, and one is soda powder. But they're all white. How can you tell the difference?" Since I was preparing for a chemistry test the next day, I took a very academic perspective on his question. As I washed my teacher's back I tried to come up with a good answer. Eventually he asked if I'd figured it out and I admitted that I hadn't. His question was a difficult challenge. When my teacher finally got out of the bath, calling me by my ordination name, he asked me, "Gensho, have you figured it out yet?"

"No sir," I said.

My teacher shook his head. "You would know if you tasted it."

At the time, I thought this was just a funny moment, but later as I studied Buddhism and began my Zen training, I realized how much importance Zen places on concreteness. Then I was able to understand how good my first master's teachings were for a young monk.

I was very fond of my teacher, even though he was strict and severe. While I was still in junior high, just hearing his voice made me quake, but eventually I got used to it. My first teacher was also a very open person. Even if he was angry one moment, the next he would turn and ask someone for tea. By the time I entered college, I understood this to be simply how he was. He could be angry one minute and smile the next. Since I realized this and was very fond of him, when I became head monk with five disciples under me, I taught them in the same way. For the younger disciples who came after me, not only was the master severe, I was too.

If my first master got along well with someone, he'd be forthright about how he felt. But if a visitor he didn't like came to the temple, he'd say so and have the vice resident priest meet that person. My second master would never do such a thing; my second master got along with everyone. I try to be more like my second master in that way. My first master's personality was very straightforward, maybe a little like Americans who tend to be very direct about saying yes or no.

My first master was physically really huge for a Japanese person. I'm personally small, even for a Japanese person. The first time I washed his back I said, "Master, your back is huge!" He said, "Big is best!" Hearing this and being small, I was worried I'd never be a great Zen master. Then during my third year in high school, the man who'd later become my second master came to the temple. My first master and I went to the temple gate to receive him. My teacher praised this man who would later become my second master as we waited. I imagined how he would look. Given that my master, who was huge, respected him, I thought he'd be huge too.

We stood waiting as the taxi approached. I was told to open the door for the visiting teacher if he was on my side, and fortunately he was. I was nervous. I made a deep bow and opened the door of the taxi. A voice from just above my head said, "Thank you." My first master would never say that. I looked up in surprise and saw that this teacher was my size. After meeting him, I knew I too could be a great Zen master.

All human beings are different. If all monks became Zen masters, that would be fine. But it's a long, rigorous route, so most monks stop part way. The standard now is that monks must spend at least three years in the monastery after university to become priests. Then they go to local temples and become the priests of those temples. Their training may not yet have culminated in a great satori enlightenment, but they've gotten the basics down to live as priests and continue training. This allows them to deepen their own practice and to serve people in their communities. It's fine that there are different ways of doing things.

Deciding how far to pursue training is a matter of individual choice. Shakyamuni Buddha appears to be the complete example of enlightenment. I myself give all my energy to the training of my disciples. Some monks give their all and some monks practice half-heartedly. Anyone who gives himself up completely to training may be able to attain the same state as his teacher, but it requires a tremendous amount of energy to do it, so most don't or can't. A Zen master tries to take each person as far as he can and in the best way he can.

There are individual differences and that's fine. It was a great encouragement for me to see with my own eyes two fine Zen masters—what a human being can attain. But even if a teacher exhausts himself to train a disciple, the disciple must also exhaust himself. In any case, for both of them, disciple and master, the deepening of awakening continues until death, reaching new levels of enlightenment, new ways to respond to life and to the world.

Rinzai Zen Monastic Training

The realization of no-self requires severe training and
Zen monastic training is quite difficult.

A MONASTERY IS a greenhouse for growing no-ego. There are
thirty-nine Rinzai monasteries in Japan at present. In a Japanese
Rinzai monastery, each monk is given one thin sleeping cushion
and one tatami mat as his personal space. The sleeping cushion is
folded in half and the monk lies on it to sleep. There is no soft pillow
for the monk's head. It only takes about three minutes from the end
of zazen for everyone to lie down. By 9:05 or 9:07 every night, in
every one of the thirty-nine Rinzai zendos, all the monks are lying
down in the way I've described. Of course, if monks were actually
able to sleep from 9:00 PM on—even given the thin cushions—we
could say the monastery was a paradise. But the fact is that they
cannot sleep.

As soon as the lights go out at 9:07, the monks get up one by one
and find their way onto a veranda outside the chanting hall. Every
monk must do this. This is when night sitting begins. The night sitting period is not limited by clappers or by other signals, nor is it just a
single sitting period. Everyone is expected to sit for at least one hour. It
is permissible, if one wishes, to sit all night until the 3:00 AM wake-up
the following day. How a monk's Zen abilities develop depends on

how he uses this night sitting period. So goes the daily routine in a monastery.

In every monastery there is, of course, a Zen master. The only time most monks meet the master directly is during koan question-and-answer periods. But during the normal course of the daily practice routine, the Zen master is able to look at all the monks at some point. First there are the senior monks. The Zen master teaches the senior monks, and it's the senior monks' job to teach the middle- and most junior-grade monks. This turns out to be a rather effective method of training. But sometimes the master will come into direct contact with a new monk. When monks walk through the monastery, they must hold their hands in a particular position and walk as though they were cats. Personally speaking, if I encounter a new monk and he's holding his hands in a sloppy position or his walking is too noisy, I don't hesitate to scold him. Everyone tries to walk quietly, but new monks unconsciously make noise when they walk the wooden hallways. When I encounter a new monk making too much noise walking, I scold him in a loud voice. So in one way or another the Zen master oversees daily life in the monastery.

The monastic way of life is designed to encourage monks to continue their training. As for myself, I am a big joker. If I think a monk has a relaxed way about him, I might play a joke on him. In the monastery, monks aren't expected to laugh so hard their teeth show. On the other hand, the Zen master can laugh however he wishes. Sometimes, I'll tell a joke and cause a monk to crack up, but he must contain himself until he has walked away a bit. Then he can laugh. This joking is just one form of personal encouragement.

An American student asked me if the head abbot in a training monastery has loving concern for the daily care of his spiritual sons. The answer is yes. But if this is so, he went on to ask, shouldn't the abbot let sleepy monks sleep? The answer is no. Monks in a training monastery have special needs. In this sense laypeople and training monks are different. In another sense, laypeople and monks equally share the possibility of attaining enlightenment and both have primary buddha nature. But just as there are professionals and amateurs in the world of sports, in Buddhism you could say that laypeople are amateurs and training monks and nuns are professionals. And since it is our duty to train the monks, it's essential that we provide a professional level of training.

There are fifteen monks in my monastery. All of the monks are trying to realize no-self, but each monk has his own individual characteristics. We respect this. Some are sharp, some are not so sharp. Some are fast, some are slow. The aim is to be aware of others and try to match the situation, to fit in, rather than judge—to function with no-self. If one could elevate this way of no-self to a national scale, it would be quite something.

In any case we don't let the monks sleep much, and we limit them to simple food. They always want to sleep more, but this is just another illusion. And because they're always eating simple food, they're always craving richer food. And this, too, is just another illusion. But such illusions are simple. There are other kinds of illusions that are much more complicated. So we focus on these two very simple illusions to ward off more complicated illusions. This is part of the wisdom of our long Zen tradition. Perhaps you feel sorry for sleepy, hungry-looking monks, but if you let them sleep and eat more, their illusions will proliferate, so we train them in the opposite direction. That's how we see things.

The realization of no-self requires severe training and Zen monastic training is quite difficult. It's not just strict, it's excessive; monks get up at three every morning every day of the year and often practice until eleven at night. There is no rest and there are no holidays during the year. On average we do six hours a day of zazen, but for a monk serious about training, six hours a day of zazen is insufficient. It's essential to deepen the monks' experiential understanding of Zen itself. This is the focus of the direct koan question-and-answer sessions each morning and evening. But these sessions alone aren't enough. During the year there are seven sesshins (intensive trainings) of seven days each. During sesshin monks stop cleaning, begging, and working in the fields. We just do hour-long periods of zazen, one after the other. For six of the seven training periods, we get about three hours of sleep a night. But during the final seven-day sesshin of the year, there is no sleeping.

When I myself first did this seven-day sesshin without sleep, I thought it was strange. Frankly I thought it was crazy. Even after becoming a Zen master and engaging in this kind of training year after year, I still think it's fair, from the standpoint of normal human life, to call it strange that nobody lies down to sleep for seven days. But there are illusions you simply cannot remove without this kind of severe training. Engaging in this kind of severe training greatly increases one's Zen power. There are many examples of people gaining satori during this severe final training period each December. My master Shibayama Roshi was such a case. I would never say this in Japan, but I too have had this experience. And based on my own personal experience, I know that anyone can experience this satori even though it is really very difficult and nearly impossible.

Having the experience of Mu involves great internal change, and the external world you see changes as well. When you speak to others who have had the same experience, you can say that the tree you saw yesterday is different from the tree you see today. You can say the pine tree in the garden is shining and someone who has had the experience will understand what you mean, but it will make no sense to someone who hasn't.

Gaining satori and experiencing Mu means that for a brief moment one spiritually dies. This fact of losing one's self is very important. While spiritually becoming Mu means undergoing a kind of death, there is also a return or a revival. You could say that when you die, you live—but this is something you have to experience for yourself. With the personal experience of Mu, a new self is born.

Without this kind of death and rebirth, Zen would be a dead religion.

A Thief Comes to Tofukuji

Because Zen emphasizes that you must become what you encounter, when you encounter something enjoyable, it's very enjoyable, and when you encounter something sad, it's okay to cry.

DAILY LIFE based on mushin is a very free existence. In English we use the words *freedom* and *free*; in Chinese the term for freedom was originally a Zen term composed of two characters. The first character means "myself" and the second character means "to depend upon." Thus the meaning of freedom—*jiyu,* in Chinese—means to depend upon oneself. If one only understands freedom superficially, one might mistakenly think it means dependence upon an egotistical existence. But if we fully understand freedom we know it is a Zen expression. We must ask, "What is the self upon which we must depend?" We depend on the self that arises when we destroy our ego. Because we depend upon this no-ego self, existence is quite free. I can say this from personal experience: when the ego is destroyed, and when we can adapt to and respond to anything and everything and accept everything, the heart feels spacious.

Until I trained as a Zen monk, I had a reputation for being rather hard-nosed. In my native temple, I would often get mad at the younger monks beneath me, probably because I had a strong ego. My third year of training was very important for me. When I returned to my native temple during the fourth year of my training, one of the younger monks remarked that I didn't get as mad as I used to anymore. It was only when he said this that I realized I had changed. When you enter mushin, you get mad less often.

You could also say you become very happy. But just because you feel happy doesn't mean you'll be overjoyed with everything that happens. If there's an earthquake, you're not happy about it. When you encounter something unfortunate, you're saddened by it. But because Zen emphasizes that you must become what you encounter, when you encounter something enjoyable, it's very enjoyable, and when you encounter something sad, it's okay to cry.

In my monastery only my quarters have television. Monks are not permitted to watch television or read newspapers. The monks' ability to see into themselves is sharpened by eliminating TV and newspapers. One is allowed to read newspapers when one reaches one's fifth year and becomes a senior monk. As a Zen master I have to read newspapers and watch television. This is because I often have to leave the monastery to lecture to laypeople. So I need to be aware of what's going on in the world.

My work with the monks on their Zen koans ends at five in the morning. I'd like to watch TV after I finish, but there's no TV in Japan at five in the morning. A friend of mine works at NHK, the Japanese TV network. I told him, "You guys sleep too much," but he replied, "No, you get up too early." So I set up satellite TV for the abbot's quarters. There are twenty-five subtemples on the Tofukuji grounds, which means there are twenty-five priests—one for each subtemple. But I was the first to get satellite TV because I have to know about the world.

When a famous drama is on TV, many people watch it, so sometimes I find sources for my lectures in TV dramas. Because I'm a very happy man, when I come across a sad drama, there's nothing to do but cry. And sometimes a handkerchief isn't enough, so I need to keep a big towel nearby to wipe away my tears when I'm watching a sad drama. I mentioned this once in a lecture and a member of the audience asked me after the talk why Zen masters cry. I answered that it's *because* I'm a Zen master that I cry. Fully taking anything in means when you're happy, you're very happy, and when you're sad, you cry. To understand about the difference between before training and after training is to understand that after training one is not so attached to one's feelings; one is free to experience them.

Freedom of mind is born from mushin. Even though there's nothing binding me, this is not a passive freedom, not a freedom *from*, but a freedom *to*. You go forward freely, but this is not a selfish freedom, it is not self-centered freedom. Basically, a Mu person cannot be self-centered or selfish. You naturally begin to think of everyone around you and to love people around you. Loving and self-examination arise naturally. If you throw your ego away, you naturally think about and love people around you from the bottom of your heart. If you cut off your ego, you experience this love arising with no explanation. This is the true Mu experience. This is good understanding.

Compassion is different from romantic love. While I don't deny the beauty of romantic love, compassionate action is the expression of religious love. Romantic love is very beautiful, especially in the beginning. For the lovers involved there is no problem. However, there may be a problem for other people around them, who may feel left out. What's more, romantic love can become egotistical, greedy, or selfish. But religious love arises from the religious and spiritual "conversion experience" of becoming the Mu self. In order to experience this kind of religious or spiritual love, you have to be able to forget yourself. To put this even more strongly, in a situation where you need to save an infant in front of a car, in that moment, you forget yourself completely to save the baby. This is the religious love that arises with the Mu experience. Compassion has many forms.

Six years ago a man named M. came to visit Tofukuji. Mr. M. was not a friend of mine. In fact, he was a thief, and I have no thieves as friends. Anyway, this fellow came to the temple and said he wanted to meet me. A senior monk led him to the guest receiving room. When I entered the receiving room, this young man introduced himself, announcing that his name was M., that he was thirty years old, and that he was a thief. I got very, very mad. I have a loud voice and M. was so taken aback, he fell into a chair. I was mad because thief is not an occupation.

Earlier, when the senior monk was leading him to the guest room, Mr. M. had asked what he should do when the roshi came into the room and the monk told him he should just introduce himself; simply give his name, age, and occupation. I'm sure Mr. M. had never been given an opportunity to introduce himself as a thief. So this introduction was a first for M. You have to admit he was honest. He really had no other work.

After initially getting mad I spoke with him. When M. left the monastery, he decided to go directly to the police, and he's in prison even now. I think he is scheduled to be released soon. It may be difficult for him to reenter society. After all he's now roughly thirty-six years old. In any case when he leaves prison, if he comes to speak to me about becoming a priest, I'd be happy to have him train with me. Two or three years from now, I may return here with M. to give another lecture.

Before M. left he asked me one question. He said, "When I first introduced myself to you, you got really mad. You're really a scary fellow. But a minute later, you spoke kindly to me. How can you change your feelings so quickly?" Intentionally bringing anger forward and then letting go of it completely in the next moment is something a Zen master who has experienced satori enlightenment can do. Because of the satori experience, you are able to live a free daily life.

13

Experiencing Enlightenment

Shibayama Roshi, convinced he might have lost his
mind, heard the birds. He thought, "Ah, the birds are
singing." But he realized there is no self that listens—
a good experience of Zen.

IN JAPAN ZEN MASTERS never talk about what they experience
regarding enlightenment, but in the West—where Zen is just beginning to take root—it's acceptable to do so. Someone asked me about
this a year ago and I answered. Personally I don't really want to discuss the topic in terms of "Hey, I got satori!" When you teach, you
don't want to give off this kind of smell—the "stink of Zen"—that
you're somehow great because you attained enlightenment. I stress
this emphatically to Westerners. There are many people in American Zen centers who say such things about themselves. In Japan
it's a tradition that Zen masters themselves never speak about their
own enlightenment and their own positions. But it might be wise to
actually explain this to Americans. So as a special offering, I'll tell
you about what my master Shibayama Roshi experienced.

Shibayama Roshi didn't mention his own experience until he was
past the age of seventy. No one asked him about it and he spoke about
it only once at a meeting for laypeople. By chance I was his attendant
monk at the time. In the monastery no one would talk about such a
thing, so this was the first time I heard such a story. He had had his

first major experience during a Rohatsu sesshin—the most intensive retreat week of the year—in his third year of training as a monk. To put the experience simply, we could say it's an experience in which you become Mu. You don't disappear physically and become nothing; rather, while you are alive, you realize you are no-thing.

Just before you have this experience, without fail some kind of illusion arises. And for each individual, the particular illusion is different. Shibayama Roshi was sitting zazen. Nearby there was another temple that would ring a large bell at eight o'clock each evening. Shibayama Roshi heard the sound and thought, "Ah, the bell is ringing." When you sit zazen, your eyes are half open and half shut. When Shibayama Roshi heard the gong, he said it was as though the sound waves turned into a gold thread, which he could see before his eyes. He thought this was strange.

The bell rang again, and again he could see the wave. He thought maybe he'd lost something. So he opened his eyes and looked across the zendo and saw the other monks in zazen. He felt he shouldn't let something so insignificant disturb him, so he lowered his eyes to resume zazen. At this point the golden thread disappeared, but it was followed by another illusion.

One day on begging rounds, Shibayama Roshi saw a parent and child begging. They were extremely dirty. These days you don't see such things in Japan. But when Shibayama Roshi was training in Kyoto, you would sometimes see such beggars. He thought that among all the beggars he'd ever seen, never had he seen beggars as dirty as this pair. He thought they were so dirty that they were Zen masters of begging. This was how desperate they were. They made a very strong impression on him. This is what came to him as an illusion during his zazen. But in the illusion the beggars were wearing clothes of gold. Shibayama Roshi thought he had gone a little bonkers.

Then he thought even if he went crazy, he would continue. You can see he was practicing at a very high level. I was moved when I heard this story. Shibayama Roshi sat like that through the night. The next morning he forgot which day of the week it was, having been without sleep, as is customary during Rohatsu sesshin. The monastery was surrounded by woods, so when dawn came, all the birds began singing together. Sitting at dawn you can feel this. The birds are sparrows. Shibayama Roshi, convinced he might have lost his mind, heard the birds. He thought, "Ah, the birds are singing." But he realized there is no self that listens—a good experience of Zen.

For those who truly understand Zen, we can say it is the no-self that hears the sparrows. That morning they served tea. When he drank it, he thought, "Ah, this tea is very good." But he also realized it is the no-self that drinks the tea. He had the experience of the no-self drinking. This is the experience of becoming Mu, or nothing.

After this Shibayama Roshi went to Zen question and answer. His master looked at him and could see Shibayama Roshi had had a deep experience. But one must not make a mistake. This is just a first experience. In terms of koan study, Shibayama Roshi had just done a little bit. He still had two thousand questions left to cover, and through the study of these koans, you deepen your understanding. This is somewhat misunderstood in America. Many people believe that when you have just this first experience, that's it, that's the great satori enlightenment experience. Of course there's a great difference between whether you have such an experience or not. But you have to deepen this experience up until the time of death.

This was Shibayama Roshi's first experience of enlightenment, and because I was so greatly moved hearing about it I wanted to talk about it. When I returned to the monastery, I gathered together all the monks who hadn't heard the story, and to encourage them, I told them the story. I told them Shibayama Roshi's experience was wonderful because he had a lot of gold images. In my own experience there was no image of gold. The illusions that bothered me included a vision of mercury. I wondered why the master had gold and I only had silver. In terms of illusions you get all sorts of colors.

What I want you to understand is that to have this first experience, you have to pass through a rather dangerous spiritual phase. In the old days monks who weren't mentally stable might develop mental problems at this phase. But if your spiritual power is strongly supported by sincere intention, you'll get through it.

14

Master Shibayama's Teaching on Beyond Words

My seventy-year-old master immediately stood up and said, "That's not the Awa dance. This is!" And he danced the Awa dance. This is an example of teaching beyond words.

ZEN IS SAID TO BE a teaching "beyond words." Sometimes it is expressed as "not relying on words and letters." There is a profound meaning to the term "beyond words." We shouldn't understand it to mean that transcending words means to remain silent. In Chinese, the term is expressed with just one Chinese character that includes graphs for both words and letters, which means something like "writings."

What does it really mean to not depend on words and letters? It's not about negating words and letters. Attachment to words and letters is what is negated. Words and letters live in the domain of intellectual knowledge, so to transcend words and letters means to transcend intellectual knowledge. Not relying on words and letters doesn't mean not using them. On the contrary it means using words and letters with true freedom. Zen has always emphasized freedom from attachment to words and letters. I think modern people are especially attached to words and letters. Perhaps this is one reason people in the West are becoming interested in Buddhism and Zen.

As people become aware of their attachment to words and letters, they recognize a need to transcend that attachment.

All intellectual knowledge is based on a kind of duality or dualistic opposition. When I was fourteen, I became an acolyte monk at my home temple. It was a large temple complex with about twenty subtemples within the monastery compound. One of the subtemples had an elderly Zen priest who was rather severe. At one point my master sent me to his temple to tend to some business. My master told me, "This guy's a real S.O.B., so be careful." My master said if I didn't bow deeply to the old priest when I met him, I'd be in real trouble. I was nervous about this, and sure enough when I arrived, a growly looking old guy came out of the temple. But he didn't look severe to me at all. This was because he was holding his grandson in his arms and this seemed to have put him in a gentle mood. I saw a kind and gentle old man.

I thought, "If that's his grandson, there must be a father somewhere." Sure enough, behind the old priest was the father, the old priest's son. The old priest held up his grandson and said, "Isn't he a beautiful baby? He looks just like me, doesn't he? Looks like he'll be intelligent when he grows up, doesn't he?" The father was there in the background, but not a word about him. To me, the baby looked more like a baby monkey, and because I was disarmed by the old priest's gentle mood, I spoke frankly and said, "He doesn't look so smart to me. He looks more like a little monkey."

The old priest replied, "No! He's very smart!" and set the baby down on the tatami mat. Zen priests usually carry a formal fan. The old priest started playing with his fan, waving it over the baby's face and asking, "What color is it? What color is it?" Of course at that age, the baby couldn't know it was red. The baby burped, and his grandfather immediately remarked, "He said 'Red'!" He turned the fan over to the other side, which was white, and continued to wave it asking, "What color is it?" And the baby, not knowing a thing about color, let out another sound, whereupon his grandfather said, "See! What did I tell you? He said 'White.'"

That's intellectual knowledge for you. The act of discriminating between red and white is an example of making an intellectual distinction. When you're born, when you're an infant, you're beyond words; you can't make such a distinction. Developing the intellect means developing the ability to discriminate and developing the ability to speak about it. This is the process of intellectualization. I don't mean to criticize intellectual knowledge. I myself am something of an intellectual scholar-monk who undertook graduate studies at the university. And I'm not taking intellectual knowledge lightly, either. From the perspective of everyday life, the distinctions we make seem absolute to us. But as the expression "beyond words" suggests, there's a reality beyond our discrimination. Zen teaches us to overcome our attachment to intellectual knowledge and transcend dualistic discrimination.

By way of example I'll tell you a story about Fuketsu, a Tang dynasty Zen master. A monk came to Fuketsu and asked, "If you cannot speak and cannot remain silent, what do you do?" This question clearly seeks that which is beyond words. Fuketsu responded, "I always remember Konan, south of the Yangtze River, early spring, the partridges singing in a mountain full of flowers." This is actually two lines from a famous poem written by the Buddhist poet Toho, Case 24 of the *Mumonkan*. Fuketsu's response was free verbal expression. The point is that to go beyond words, one must be able to use words freely. Master Fuketsu could also have responded by remaining silent. You can see that Zen is a religion and teaching beyond words.

A great deal of Zen monastic training is beyond words. I do give Zen lectures, but the monks don't engage in academic study. In fact their daily life is largely beyond words. I tell Westerners who come to train in my monastery that they don't need to learn Japanese because Zen training is quite literally beyond words. In Rinzai Zen we do koan question-and-answer study and this takes place morning and evening almost every day. Koans are brief and concise, but there's real teaching going on and American disciples are able to do it with me in English. This fundamental training is beyond words, even though we do use words.

For example, here's a relatively difficult koan: "You cannot express it positively. Nor can you do it negatively. Neither the negative nor the positive will do. At such a point, what do you do?" If there's any intellectual functioning going on in working with this koan, you can't grasp it. I myself was stuck on this koan for an entire week of intensive training. I was meeting with my master five times a day for seven days. In all I wrestled with this koan thirty-five times during the course of the week. Finally I said to my master, "This is nonsense." Nonsense is beyond words. My master said, "Show me a Zen answer that is nonsense." So I stood up and danced. He asked, "What kind of dance is that?" I was actually trying to do a famous dance from Shikoku in Japan called the Awa dance, and that's what I told him. At this point my seventy-year-old master immediately stood up and said, "That's not the Awa dance. This is!" And he danced the Awa dance. This is an example of teaching beyond words.

After our exchange my master told me I should go to Tokushima where they do the Awa dance and see how it's done. Finally, eight years later, I found time to go. When we were in koan dokusan, I thought my master did the dance quite well. Now I'm not so sure. In Tokushima at the Awa Festival, I watched them dance over the course of two nights. While they're dancing, they sing this song, "I'm a dancing fool, you're a dancing fool, we're all fools; let's dance."

I was a Zen master so I couldn't be out there dancing, but I did watch carefully.

Later I went to visit my master's grave—he had since passed away—to pay my respects to him. I didn't dance in front of his grave, but I did say, "I can now do the Awa dance better than you."

15

Severe Training

Even if you are missing a leg or even missing two legs,
you can still sit in zazen.

AFTER LEARNING of the story of Bokuju and Ummon (see chapter 32), I came to believe that even if it meant losing your leg or both your hands, that's how badly you should want to gain satori enlightenment. My master in the training monastery at that time encouraged me very much. He told me to stake my very life on practice. When you put your life on the line to gain awakening, it has great meaning. Trying to sit the night sitting as hard as you can, you do come to believe you should put your life on the line. So I thought even if you lost your hands or your legs, you should try to get satori enlightenment.

Later I reflected on this period of training and realized my way was not quite complete. In China there was a Zen master by the name of Funyo. Whenever Funyo fell asleep, he would take a sharp awl and stick himself in the leg to wake himself up. This is a pretty tough practice. Knowing the story, I thought perhaps I should give it a try. I didn't have an awl but I did have a knife, so I decided to use that. If I fell asleep, I imagined, I would take up the knife and stick myself in the leg. But I really couldn't bring myself to stick myself hard; I just kind of pricked myself. I realized just how hard it is to put your life on the line for something.

During my training I thought over and over about Ummon's story and his broken leg. While Ummon had a very great satori understanding, he also ended up with only one leg. Now whenever I talk about zazen in Japan, just as I am explaining here, I say that one should cross one's legs only to the point that one can. Even in Japan there are many people who mistakenly think that if you cannot sit in full lotus, you cannot sit in zazen. Some people believe that since they cannot cross their legs, they should not go to zazen retreats. But that's not the way it is. Ummon himself was able to sit with only one leg. Even if you are missing a leg or even missing two legs, you can still sit in zazen. Ummon was able to complete his training in just such a fashion.

In the monastery the monks are sleepy all day long and this is something we do on purpose. It's the same when it comes to food. In the morning the monks eat pickled plums and gruel. At lunch, it's rye gruel with miso soup and pickles. It's the same at night. Monastery meals are simple for the sake of spiritual practice. Simple food is best, even though I'm sure the monks would like to eat more delicious food. And since they don't get to sleep much, they're always sleepy. During meditation difficult thoughts arise, but in this sleepy, hungry condition, unnecessary illusions don't appear quite so easily. This is a very efficient practice.

No matter how you look at it, Zen monastery training emphasizes experiential training, which is why monks are encouraged to study in college before entering a monastery. There's no paper test to enter a Zen monastery. But there is a spiritual test. To begin with you have to sit for two days on the steps at the main entrance to the monastery. This is physically stressful. Sitting on the steps requires twisting your body and putting your head down for the entire day in a way that is quite tiring. Still, anyone can bear it for a couple of days.

Almost thirty years ago, I went through this process myself. During the course of the morning of the first day, I was so covered with sweat that my straw sandals became quite damp. It was tough, but bearable for the two days. Twice a day a senior monk comes and throws you out of the monastery, but you have to come right back, sit down, and put your head down again. When the two days finish, you then spend five days sitting alone in a small room, facing the wall. Spiritually speaking, the five days are much tougher. You have all sorts of experiences over the course of those five days. You could say it's a process of throwing out everything that's ever happened to you before. Of course you can't throw out everything; but for the next two or three years in the monastery, you continue looking inward and throwing away whatever arises.

When I entered Nanzenji monastery, I sat and faced the wall for five days. In one corner, low on the wall, I discovered that some monk who'd been there before me had written some graffiti. This is not something a monk should do, and there's always someone looking in on you while you're there. I have no idea who did it. But what was written was very effective for those sitting in the room. The graffiti said, "Forget." While written minutely, over the course of five days of sitting, eventually you'll find it.

After the seven days—two at the entrance and five facing the wall—on the morning of the eighth day, you're invited to meet the Zen master himself. Now that I am a Zen master, every spring new monks come to the monastery. When a monk finally comes to meet me, he makes a deep bow before me. There's a bit of distance between us. While the monk is in this deep bowing posture, he must listen to his first teaching. I always ask the monks to raise their heads. This is because I want to check their eyes. After the monks have gone through the seven-day entering process, you can see in their eyes a certain determination to continue with the training. If they don't have such a spirit, they're not accepted into the monastery. Without this kind of fundamental spiritual power, a monk won't survive in the monastery.

In any discussion of monastic life, its severe aspects are apparent. The severity is designed for monks who've chosen to enter priestly life. It's only natural that monks would undergo severe monastic training, but the way of teaching laypeople is quite different. Upon entering the monastery, monks begin a routine of getting up at three in the morning and going to bed at nine at night. Life continues in this way throughout the year. The monks always begin the day with an hour of chanting. At 4:15 AM, there's a simple breakfast. Lunch and dinner are also quite simple. Zazen begins at 4:30 and continues through the day until dark. Sitting time varies, depending on the season. In any case, zazen periods are each one hour long. At the start of the first period in the morning, there is always Zen question and answer. Once dawn breaks, all the monks engage in cleaning the buildings and the surrounding grounds. When this is finished, they go out on begging rounds. This commences about 7:30 AM in the winter; a bit earlier in the summer months.

As for begging rounds, methods differ between city and country monasteries, but the spiritual nature is the same. Monks must be back to the monastery by 10:00 AM. They are broken into two groups for lunch, which begins at 10:30 and wraps up at 11:00. Lunch is followed by a break until 1:00, during which the monks can write postcards, do laundry, etc. But nobody is to talk about unnecessary things or lie down to rest. Books are limited to two: a lecture book used for Zen lectures and a koan phrase book. For monks who have no particular activities to take care of, it's best to just sit and do zazen during breaks. There's also a short break just after dinner. A monk's ability to live and survive in the monastery depends on how he uses these breaks.

Manual labor begins at one o'clock, when the break ends, and concludes at 4:30 PM. Dinner begins at 4:45. After sunset, the monks gather in the zendo. At sunset, the official signal starts zazen. At this time there's a second question-and-answer period with the Zen master. These koan question-and-answer sessions are thus scheduled just twice a day—once in the morning and once in the evening. Zazen continues until 9:00 PM. At that time, two short prayers are read for Mañjuśrī Bodhisattva, who's enshrined in the zendo. Finally, the lights are turned out.

16

Koan Practice

Joshu could just as well have answered "A" or "B."
He could have answered "S" for St. Louis. He could
have answered anything. All he had to do was convey
his own buddha nature directly.

THERE ARE TWO MAJOR SECTS in Japanese Zen: the Rinzai sect,
to which I belong, and the Soto sect. There's also the Obaku sect,
which is an historic offshoot of the Rinzai sect. In Japan in the Rinzai
sect, we practice both sitting meditation and koans, but in Soto, they
practice only sitting meditation. American Zen is different because
they study koan questions in Soto Zen centers. I think this is fine for
American Zen.

Koans came from China to Japan and now have reached the West.
I am convinced that Westerners do not need new koans. The koan
is a Zen question. The question is not satori enlightenment but a
method for attaining satori enlightenment. Sometimes people try to
master koans through the intellect, but koan practice is an experiential endeavor.

There are 1,700 koans, and if you include all the subquestions
the number grows to 3,000. Among the 3,000, there are two fundamental koans. The first has 102 subquestions and the second has
94. Thus about 200 koans are associated with the two fundamental koans. When a Japanese Zen monk studies these first 200, he

establishes the foundation of his Zen experience. This typically takes three to six years. If we say a monk does it in three years, finishing all 3,000 would theoretically take forty-five years. But it actually takes more like ten to fifteen years because as a monk progresses, his experience deepens and it gets easier to give a good answer the first time. By the time he gets to the last hundred koans, he's able to give the correct answer the first time every time.

But simply completing all the koan questions doesn't qualify a monk as a Zen master. That's just the first requirement. Afterward the monk must leave the monastery and practice on his own without the guidance of a master. We call this period of time "special training." It's very important and takes about another ten years. This special training has two goals. The first is to deepen one's Zen experience on one's own. The second is to develop a personality worthy of a Zen master. During this period outside the monastery, the monk returns a few times a year to have his progress checked by his master. Only when a disciple has attained a depth of Zen mind and a good personality adequate for a Zen master does his master allow him to be called Zen master. So in Rinzai Zen in Japan, it takes about twenty years to become a Zen master. We're very careful about this.

The first fundamental koan is Joshu's Mu. In brief it begins as follows: A monk asked Joshu, "Does that dog have buddha nature or not?" Why did the monk ask about a dog? He could have asked about a cat or a tiger. But Zen is concrete. In India Buddhism was philosophical, but in China Buddhism became concrete, practical, and pragmatic, so Zen questions are very concrete. So we can assume that at that very moment there was a dog walking in front of him. He pointed and asked, "Does that dog have buddha nature?" Joshu replied, "Mu." That's why this is called the Mu koan.

The question is a good one. In China at that time, monks were familiar with the *Nirvana Sutra*, the main teaching of which was "all beings have primary buddha nature." So the monk's question to Joshu is related to this *Nirvana Sutra* teaching. If Joshu had said "No," the monk would have thought it conflicted with the *Nirvana Sutra's* main teaching. If Joshu had answered, "Yes, the dog does have buddha nature," the monk would have asked why, in that case, it was an animal.

But the true meaning of the question is not whether or not the dog has buddha nature. The *Nirvana Sutra* states plainly that all beings do, including animals and plants. It includes all of nature. So of course the dog has buddha nature. The true meaning of the koan is "What is buddha nature?" and to this Joshu replied, "Mu."

Mu can be translated as "no," but in this case it doesn't mean that the dog doesn't have buddha nature. Zen Master Joshu, in his greatness, immediately understood the deeper meaning of the monk's question. By answering "Mu" Joshu was able to convey fully his own buddha nature. In another section of the *Record of Joshu*, to the same question Joshu answered "U," which is the complete opposite of Mu. But *U* in this case can't be translated simply as "yes." By merely saying the word *U*, Joshu once again completely conveyed his own buddha nature. Joshu could just as well have answered "A" or "B." He could have answered "S" for St. Louis. He could have answered anything. All he had to do was convey his own buddha nature directly. In fact there's an infinite number of ways to do this. Joshu, adept with words, revealed his own buddha nature fully using both U and Mu.

As I mentioned, the Mu koan has 102 subquestions. You can consider this metaphorically in terms of a sphere. There's a point in the center of the sphere; that central point is buddha nature. The sphere also has an infinite number of points on its surface and the subquestions are like 102 points on that surface. From each point on the surface you can draw a straight line that intersects the sphere's center. That's how the subquestions work. The first fundamental question—"What is Joshu's Mu?"—points to the central question: "What is buddha nature?"

Let me give you a few examples of the 102 Mu subquestions. Western students always like examples and I usually use the same three, picked especially for them. Traditionally Japanese temples have been built with large wooden pillars. Keeping that in mind, here's a first Mu subquestion example: "Enter that pillar." That's an easy one. Here's a second example: "Two people are walking when it suddenly begins to rain, but only one gets wet. Why?" This is also an easy example. At one university where I spoke, a professor of religion said he had the answer. I invited him to share it and he said, "One had an umbrella." That's a typical bad answer. Think about it. If two people are walking together and it started to rain, and one had an umbrella, they'd share! The professor's answer is a poor one and shows that he lacked a sense of compassion.

Here's a third example. "It's not affirmative. It's not negative. It's neither affirmative nor negative. What is it?" This is a tough one and it's a good one for intellectual people. At Harvard, when they asked for a koan example, I gave them this one. Everyone in the audience thought about it, but as long as you think about it, you'll never get to the right answer. If you come to my monastery in Japan, I'll tell you the right answer in secret.

Just kidding.

17

Rough and Ready Zen

I have to say those Tang dynasty Chinese Zen masters were really quite rough and ready.

THERE ARE MANY Zen stories about the transcendence of dualism. For example, there came a time when Zen Master Hyakujo had
to choose a successor. There were about eight hundred monks studying under him at the time. In order to pick his successor, one day
Hyakujo set a water pitcher down on the ground in front of him and
said to his disciples: "This is a water pitcher on the ground. Do not
call it a water pitcher. What do you call it?" The head monk responded
immediately saying, "Well, I sure wouldn't call it a piece of wood."
This a pretty good answer that shows the transcendence of dualism.
The head monk was not attached to the form of the water pitcher
as a water pitcher. Hyakujo then asked his disciple Isan, "What do
you have to say about this?" Isan immediately went up and knocked
over the pitcher. Needless to say Hyakujo passed on his succession
to Isan.

The head monk's response was good, but compared with Isan's
kicking over the pitcher, you can see that the head monk's Zen
understanding is still incomplete. The head monk was still somewhat attached to the dualistic question of whether or not to call it
a pitcher. Isan's response went beyond the dualism of calling the
pitcher this or that or anything at all; with total freedom, Isan kicked

the pitcher over. We can see how great Isan's answer was from the perspective of transcending dualism.

Looking back to the time of the Tang dynasty over a thousand years ago, we could say that the monks of that era went too far in some sense. Nowadays we might think it's not really necessary to do something as rough as knocking over the pitcher. There was probably clean water available at the temple. Wouldn't it have been a perfectly suitable response to simply get up, drink some water, and say, "That's delicious?" The long development of Buddhism up to and through the Tang dynasty naturally brought it to a point where what we might call a kind of radical or extreme action revealed the truth.

Whether one names or doesn't name the pitcher, simply kicking the pitcher doesn't mean one has transcended duality. If that were the case, Zen masters would go around all day kicking things. Isan's act of knocking over the pitcher was a profound Zen act, but you have to take into account the historical and cultural circumstances of that action. Still, as a modern Zen master, I have to say those Tang dynasty Chinese Zen masters were really quite rough and ready.

The legendary Zen master Fuke lived at the same time as Zen Master Rinzai, the founder of the Rinzai sect of Zen, in a town near Rinzai's temple. Fuke had a free, unrestricted way of living without any particular dwelling. He simply came and went as he pleased. When Fuke got hungry, he'd wander over to Rinzai's temple and get some raw vegetables from the kitchen. Maybe this was the origin of the salad. Once when Fuke was eating raw vegetables in the temple kitchen, Zen Master Rinzai said to him, "You over there in the corner, chewing on raw vegetables: you look like a donkey!" Rather than responding with something like, "This is a tasty salad," or "These vegetables are good," Fuke simply brayed like a jackass. He was a good disciple, and, as you can see from this exchange, Fuke was quite free in his way.

On another occasion Fuke was resting on a bridge. I visit China each year, and each year I go to this very stone bridge near Rinzai's temple. I always remember this story. Picture Fuke resting on the stone bridge. Two monks from other Buddhist sects approach and one asks Fuke how deep he thinks the water is below the bridge. Instead of answering with something like, "Oh, about five or ten meters," Fuke grabbed the monk and threw him in the water. Not a bad Zen move! Rather than explain, let the monk get a feel for the depth of the water himself! From our contemporary point of view, this is taking things a bit too far. Instead of grabbing the other person and tossing him into the water, Fuke could have jumped into the water himself, for example. This is a matter of both the depth and the shallowness of the water and of dualism itself, isn't it?

I had an interesting experience related to this in my own life. It's a Zen story that is actually something that my master experienced and taught me about. My Zen master, Shibayama Roshi, went to visit a very good friend of his, a wealthy layperson living in a very elegant house with expansive grounds. My master went to the front entrance and called out a number of times, "Excuse me, excuse me . . .," but there was no answer. Because he was familiar with the house, he went unaccompanied around to the back. It seems the family was all the way at the back of the house and it sounded like they were having a lot of fun. He approached wondering what all the excitement was about. In fact they weren't having fun at all, but they were quite excited. My master discovered that one of the grandchildren had fallen into the well. It was an old well that was no longer in use. Apparently the grandchild had accidently slipped and fallen in. With everyone's help they were able to pull him up safely. Everyone then went to the guest room for tea and discussed what had happened.

My master asked the child, "Was the well deep?" The child answered, "It was very high." Do you understand? Looking into the well from above, we would say it is very deep. The child was looking up from below so it looked very high. Through this exchange with the child, my master came to a real understanding of the dualism of deep and shallow and high and low. Immediately upon returning to the temple, he called out to me in a loud voice, "Hey! Wells are high!" I had no idea what he was talking about, but when he explained the details, I realized what a fine story it was. From the point of view of transcending dualism, it's a very valuable story.

18

Meeting D. T. Suzuki

Zen's roots in America owe much to Suzuki's work. There are really no philosophical expressions in Zen's traditional records, but Suzuki tried to make Zen easier for Americans to understand by using such expressions.

ZEN TEACHES transcendence of dualism. That's the expression we use in English, but "transcending dualism" has a philosophical quality to it. It was D. T. Suzuki who introduced this expression. As I've mentioned previously, Indian Buddhism was very philosophical, but Chinese Buddhism, including Zen, was practical and down to earth. Chinese monks never used such terms. Suzuki purposefully introduced philosophical expressions believing that such expressions could help Western people understand Zen. He was skillful in this way.

D. T. Suzuki was a good friend of the Japanese philosopher Nishida Kitaro. They were born in the same year in Ishikawa Prefecture and were friends from early on. D. T. Suzuki was not simply a scholar; he also trained in Zen and had the same training experience that Japanese Zen monks have. But he saw himself as a scholar and chose to remain a layperson. I think if he had become a Zen monk, he would have become a great Zen master. However as a scholar, he didn't want to be called a Zen master, so in America, his title was always Dr. Suzuki. His friend Nishida Kitaro became a professor at Kyoto University where he built up a school of philosophy known as the Kyoto School. The two men had a good influence on each other. Nishida was influenced by Suzuki to develop Zen-like philosophical expressions. One example is the phrase "the contradictory identity of the self." This phrase points to how the contradictory human elements—complex and varied—become one through the self. This term "through the self" is Zen-like, because for Zen, the self is the problem. Influenced by D. T. Suzuki, Professor Nishida used expressions such as this, which are not found in the works of Heidegger or Hegel.

Professor Nishida likewise influenced D. T. Suzuki, who freely used philosophical expressions to teach Zen; the expression "transcending dualism" is just one example. After World War II, D. T. Suzuki came to America and developed and used such expressions to teach Zen to Americans. Zen's roots in America owe much to Suzuki's work. There are really no philosophical expressions in Zen's traditional records, but Suzuki tried to make Zen easier for Americans to understand by using such expressions.

I would say that D. T. Suzuki had a satori enlightenment experience. It takes a great deal of training to attain satori. Living a lay life makes it hard, but laypeople can attain satori. When he was young he trained as hard as any monk, living in a monastery in Kamakura. He did not finish all the koans; he finished half of them. There's a Zen expression, "You can twist your arm in, but you can't twist it out." D. T. Suzuki had a deep realization working with this koan, and that was his satori enlightenment experience.

After his satori experience, writing became Suzuki's form of *upaya* (skillful means). He wrote to explain what he'd come to understand. You must use whatever means or personal skills you have to express your understanding. All of D. T. Suzuki's written works are in this sense a form of upaya. I believe Suzuki got as far as the *Record of Rinzai* in his koan study and this is where you can really see the depth of his Zen understanding. His commentary on Rinzai's record is one of the very best available. It contains twenty chapters and the first sentence of the first chapter is "Zen is as it is." Someone who is just a scholar is not capable of saying such a thing. From my perspective as a Zen master, it's evident to me that Suzuki had a deep satori experience.

D. T. Suzuki also had great powers of expression. He was a professor at the college I attended and I heard him lecture for the first time when I was a freshman. I'd read his books many, many times and wondered what he'd be like in person. Wanting to get a good look at him, on the day of the lecture I found a seat in the front row. When he entered the lecture hall, I thought he looked like a monkey. There were about one thousand students there to hear him speak. He sat down and leaned against the table. In Japan to give a lecture with such an attitude is quite unthinkable. In America a professor might put his feet up on a desk when talking, but in Japan, such a thing is really out of the question.

Suzuki said nothing for quite a while. The thousand of us in the audience sat up straight, waiting, just looking at him. Perhaps two or three minutes passed. Finally Suzuki stood up and started rummaging through his pockets. He commented that he thought he'd put his lecture notes somewhere but now couldn't find them. He said, "It's okay. I have a general idea of what to say. Even without notes, I can still say something." He sat back down and began, "Zen is . . . " and from that beginning gave a wonderful lecture.

I was able to see him four more times in this same environment. The fourth time, I was a graduate student. A German scholar named Liebenthal was there as well. Professor Liebenthal had come to give a lecture about Bodhidharma, the founder of Zen in China.

Liebenthal's lecture was based on his assertion that Bodhidharma was not an actual historical figure. Only graduate students in Buddhism were allowed to attend this lecture. D. T. Suzuki was there as well. When Professor Liebenthal said Bodhidharma was not an actual historical figure, D. T. Suzuki expressed his disagreement and the lecture was followed by a very intense discussion of this matter between the two of them. Liebenthal spoke in German and another professor translated into Japanese. Suzuki spoke in Japanese, which was then translated into German. The discussion continued in this manner, growing quite intense.

Without anyone really noticing, the two had begun speaking to each other directly in English. D. T. Suzuki asserted with absolute certainty that Bodhidharma had indeed lived as a historical figure. The discussion never reached a settled conclusion, but D. T. Suzuki's abilities made a very substantial impression on the Japanese students.

19

Satori Is Not Like LSD

A Zen master must be a master. It won't do if he's
not a good, full human being.

ZEN BECAME MORE POPULAR in the West in the latter half of
the 1960s, and in 1969 I accompanied Roshi Shibayama to teach in
the West. We spent some time at a university. During the discussion
after a public lecture he'd given, a student asked him if LSD was the
medicine of enlightenment. Shibayama Roshi said it was not. The
student then asked Shibayama Roshi if he'd taken LSD himself. I
thought this was an interesting question and was very interested in
how my master would answer. Shibayama Roshi said, "Yes, I have."
But he was lying. If he'd said he hadn't, the student would have asked
him how he knew without trying it. In Japan such an exchange would
never take place. A head abbot would never be challenged in this way.
It also wouldn't happen that a head abbot would lead a retreat like
the ones we have here now. Senior monks would lead it and the head
abbot would just come for *teisho* (Dharma talks).

In any case, Shibayama Roshi said he had taken LSD. I thought
this was a rather strange and funny answer. After the lecture Shibayama Roshi told me that of course he'd lied, but so had Shakymuni
Buddha. You have to express the truth skillfully. Shibayama Roshi
said this question about LSD would likely come up over and over
among Western students, and perhaps he shouldn't have lied but

should actually try LSD. One of his disciples, a woman named Ms. Kudo, who also translated for him, begged him not to take it. Ms. Kudo said that if as head abbot he took LSD and his mind was badly affected, it would be a serious problem. If the head abbot became a crazy abbot, his disciples would be in trouble. I said I would take it in place of Shibayama Roshi. He replied jokingly that it would be no problem if I went crazy. But his translator had also trained in Zen and said neither master nor disciple should take LSD and that, as a layperson, she should be the one to take it. Again jokingly, Shibayama Roshi said that would be best. Later, having returned to Japan, she actually went through with it and took LSD.

And then there's Alan Watts. In the beginning, having studied Zen under D. T. Suzuki, Watts was a good writer. But his later books were problematic. He had become quite involved in LSD, which he brought to Kyoto. LSD was illegal in Japan at the time. Alan Watts carved a hole in a big book, put LSD in it, and brought it into Japan that way. He wanted Japanese Zen monks to take LSD so he could research the results. But this didn't happen because the Zen monks knew it was a hallucinogen. But when Shibayama Roshi's interpreter heard Watts was in Kyoto with LSD, she contacted him and told him she wanted to try it.

LSD comes in tablet form, and Ms. Kudo took a quarter of a tablet. If she'd taken the whole tablet, she might have become strange. Knowing how to do zazen, Ms. Kudo took the LSD in a small temple and sat in zazen in a quiet temple room. When you do zazen, you have to do it sitting with the feeling of being a pillar reaching all the way to heaven. Ms. Kudo had a fine sitting posture, but under the influence of the LSD, she moved around quite a bit. From time to time, one of Alan Watts's students would slide open the shoji screen and watch her. Ms. Kudo was being studied.

After taking the LSD she came to Nanzenji, Shibayama Roshi's monastery. Roshi and I were weeding the grass in one of the temple gardens. The entry to the garden was open. Ms. Kudo approached and cried out in a loud voice, "Roshi! Roshi!" She was an elegant lady who wouldn't normally shout, but we knew she had taken Alan Watts's LSD that day, and Shibayama Roshi said, "The LSD is having an effect." She was in an odd state. She said, "I've taken the LSD," speaking in an unusual way, almost as though she were singing a song. Shibayama Roshi was concerned the LSD had had too great an effect and asked her, "How was it?" The spot where Roshi and I were weeding was covered with moss and there was a camellia tree nearby with white blossoms. Ms. Kudo said the white of the flowers and the green of the moss appeared to be all mixed together. The LSD had made the colors psychedelic. Shibayama Roshi said to me, "Gen-san, it's a good thing you didn't take the LSD."

There is an expression, "The willow is green; the flower is red," and there's another expression that "The willow is not green; the flower is not red." Both are Zen expressions. In Zen it's possible to use both affirmation and negation freely. When you take LSD you can make the mistake of thinking the willow isn't green and the flower isn't red and that is satori. When hippies took LSD and experienced psychedelic phenomena, they thought their experience was the satori of Zen.

There is no real connection between Zen and the hippies, but that's how Zen appeared in the U.S. Some of these oddities have died out, and the number of Japanese-affiliated Zen centers has increased. Based on what I heard from friends, it sounded like things were moving in a positive direction. When I first returned to the States in 1989 after many years away I was a bit shocked. A version of Korean Zen meditation and Tibetan Buddhist meditation had come the U.S. and they were all kind of lumped together with Zen. And people tended to say of this kind of oriental, mystical-looking blend, "Oh, that's Zen."

I'm not saying Japanese Zen is the real thing and that Korean Zen or Tibetan Buddhism are no good. But as one professor put it, the hippie Zen of the 1960s has become a kind of tossed-salad "anything-goes Zen." As a Japanese Zen master, I feel a need to straighten out the mess. Of course, you have to make up your own minds. My job is to show what authentic Japanese Rinzai Zen is. Then it's up to the people in Western Zen centers to choose.

Religion is free, and if Westerners prefer the tossed-salad version, then so be it. Still, as a Zen master, I have to say that this may actually be a new religion; I wouldn't call it Zen. In America it's easy to become a so-called Zen master. In reality becoming a Zen master is not easy. If you compare getting a PhD to becoming a Zen master, becoming a Zen master is much harder. I'm speaking of the degree of difficulty and not meaning to suggest that a PhD is useless. A monk would need to train in a Zen monastery for at least ten years, and after that, he'd have to continue training on his own—after satori enlightenment training—and this kind of training is extremely important. This is when the monk develops fully, as a whole human being. A Zen master must be a master. It won't do if he's not a good, full human being. Only after much time and intense checking by the master is the disciple able to become a master himself.

"One Pine Is Green for One Thousand Years"

Calligraphy by Keido Fukushima

III.

Zen Master Joshu

20

Joshu, You Dirty Old S.O.B.

Zen priests respect Joshu to the point of calling him
father.

IN ZEN TRAINING one practices to realize no-self. For this purpose the Mu koan is very effective. Not just Zen masters but every
Rinzai Zen priest has to tackle this koan in the beginning of their
formal practice. When I went to China for the first time about eight
years ago, I went first to Rinzai's temple and then to Joshu's temple.
My visits to both temples were very moving. This is because among
the many Zen koans, the most basic one is the Mu koan. Joshu's Mu
is an intrinsic part of a Rinzai Zen priest's training. In this sense, all
Rinzai priests have personally met Joshu.

My first visit to Joshu's temple was with twenty other Rinzai Zen
priests. Half of the main temple hall had collapsed, and other walls
had almost totally collapsed as well. But a tower about thirty meters
high remained. This tower marked Joshu's grave. I was deeply
moved when I saw it. All the monks lined up to chant a sutra in front
of Joshu's grave.

There was one aged Zen priest among us, more than seventy
years old, who went up to the tower and started hitting the base of
the tower with both his fists. He was crying out in a very loud voice,
"This dirty old S.O.B. Joshu!" Everyone was surprised, including
me, but I quickly realized what he meant and what he was trying to

do. The old priest was in fact offering words of very high praise. A Rinzai Zen priest is only born through Joshu's Mu koan; without it there would be no Rinzai Zen priests. So we have to be very grateful to Joshu for this Mu koan. When I myself was actually trying to understand the Mu koan, I felt exactly the way the old priest did.

My own experience was that no matter how many times I tried, I never seemed to be able to answer the koan. During night sitting—I struggled with the Mu koan especially at night—I would think, "If it weren't for Joshu, there'd be no Mu." No matter how many times I brought an answer, even when I thought it was a good answer, it was wrong. Anyone who has struggled with the Mu koan knows this feeling; one really grows to dislike Joshu. Whether great or small, every Rinzai Zen priest experiences this feeling in relation to Joshu. This is why we were able to understand how the old monk felt who got mad, hit the tower, and called Joshu a dirty old S.O.B.

As the leader of the group, I read a poem of four stanzas before we chanted in front of Joshu's grave. The poem was something I'd written myself. It is traditional for the leader of the group to offer an original poem at the master's gravesite. I wrote the poem the night before, and, by chance, the poem I wrote for the occasion included this line: "I place a single lighted stick of incense before Joshu's grave, but there is no limit to what this one stick of incense contains, including a great deal of both pleasure and displeasure." When the feeling of gratitude is so great, it's not unusual to use expressions that seem to say the opposite.

I think Westerners might understand this custom. If you have a good son, for example, you might say something like, "Hey, you silly boy." Saying "You dirty old S.O.B. Joshu" is the kind of expression you would use to tease a friend. This kind of joking is an expression of affection. From ancient times, Zen monks have used this kind of opposite way of expressing praise. I also expressed in the poem I wrote the feeling of "Joshu, you dirty S.O.B." that the old monk had expressed. I had this same feeling when I wrote the poem the night before. The line was in the third part of the poem and when I read it, all of the monks began to cry. Everyone was so emotional, it was hard to distinguish whether they were chanting or crying. When the chanting finished, we turned toward the grave and made three deep bows. All twenty of us, still crying and feeling very emotional, made these deep bows.

Zen priests respect Joshu to the point of calling him father. I myself have a very special feeling for Zen Master Joshu. After visiting his temple, I often thought about meeting him. The grounds of Tofukuji, my temple in Kyoto, are quite extensive. There is a very large bridge there called Tsutenkyo, "The Bridge of Heaven." Sometimes when I'm crossing the bridge, I can't help thinking that I might meet Joshu.

21

Joshu Meets Nansen

Becoming a Zen master is not the end of practice.
One must practice as long as one lives.

JOSHU WAS A MONK of about twenty when he met Zen Master
Nansen. Nansen's temple was just south of the Yangtze River. Joshu
came from an area in northern China near present-day Beijing. He
made the long trip to southern China to practice with Nansen. The
record of their first meeting states that it was afternoon. Master Nansen was taking a nap, as was customary. Napping is a regular part of
a Chinese priest's daily schedule. I visit China every fall, and if we
visit a temple in the afternoon, the resident priest doesn't come to
greet us. Instead a young monk greets us and tells us that the resident priest is napping, would we please wait a bit. A Japanese priest
would never do that. Even if he wanted an afternoon nap, he'd go to
greet his visitors. But in China, napping is a tradition.

Joshu happened to arrive that afternoon during Zen Master Nansen's naptime. He went to Nansen's room to greet him, but instead of
getting up, Nansen remained lying down and asked Joshu, "Where
do you come from?" Joshu came from the north and could have said
so. Instead he replied, "I'm in Zen Master Nansen's temple right
now." This is a good answer. But Nansen wasn't so moved. There was
a wonderful Buddha statue at Nansen's temple and Nansen asked,
"Have you seen the wonderful Buddha statue yet?" Joshu answered,

"I have not, but I am looking at a wonderful reclining Buddha right in front of me." At this, Nansen sat up and asked, "Do you have a master?" Joshu had practiced under another master in the north, but he didn't say that. Instead, he turned to Master Nansen and asked, "How are you?" In other words he was saying, "You're my master now." This was their first meeting.

I myself have a very special feeling for Zen Master Joshu. After visiting his temple, I've often thought about meeting him.

In the town of Joshu, there was a bridge, huge for its time. Nowadays, there are big bridges everywhere. But this was built in the sixth century. The bridge forms a kind of arch. Japanese tourists these days visit and photograph the arch. The first time I saw it, I was surprised. It's wide, so wide trucks can pass each other on it. This bridge was built in the Sui dynasty and it's still famous for its architecture. And the town of Joshu is famous for this bridge.

One day, a monk came to Joshu and said to him, "I've heard of the stone bridge of Joshu and expected something big. But all I see is a tiny little wooden bridge." Actually it was a huge stone bridge. The monk was really addressing Joshu himself, using the bridge as a metaphor for Joshu's greatness. The monk was saying that compared to his reputation, Joshu was tiny.

Joshu replied, "You've only seen a tiny wooden bridge. You haven't bothered to look at the real bridge." Joshu was telling the monk that he didn't see the true Joshu. So the monk asked, "What is Joshu's bridge?" meaning "Who is Joshu really?" and Joshu answered, "Cross over, cross over."

The *Record of Joshu* says that he simply said, "Cross over, cross over." I've talked to the monks about this. While this is all he is recorded to have said, I'm sure he also became the bridge for the monk and assumed the shape of the bridge. This kind of rich expression is something a young Zen master would never come up with. Joshu's comment has a profound meaning.

This bridge story is also found in the *Blue Cliff Record*. In that version, Joshu says, "Horses can cross over, and so can donkeys." But comparing the two, I think the version in *Record of Joshu* is better: "Cross over, cross over." Anyone can cross with this answer; not only horses and donkeys, but cats, dogs, cars, anyone. This is of special significance. With "Cross over, cross over" Joshu expresses great compassion. I think of Joshu and his compassion when I cross over Tofukuji's bridge, Tsutenkyo.

Joshu was fifty-seven when his master Nansen died. For three years after Nansen's death, Joshu prayed for him. Then, when Joshu turned sixty, he started traveling around China. He traveled for twenty years. Only when he turned eighty did he settle down and become master of his own temple. Thus the records of Joshu's teaching life are drawn mostly from his life as an old Zen master. I think Zen masters need long lives. As a Zen monk, one has a first enlightenment experience and then, for the next twenty years, one continues to practice until one is ready to be a Zen master. But becoming a Zen master is not the end of practice. One must practice as long as one lives. In Zen we have a saying: "Even Shakyamuni Buddha and Bodhidharma continue to practice." Of course, both Shakyamuni Buddha and Bodhidharma are long dead. What the saying really expresses is that practice is something we must continue for our whole lives. There is a difference between a forty-year-old Zen master and a fifty-year-old Zen master. And also between them and a sixty-year-old Zen master. You must keep getting better and better. And you can't get to that point unless you live a long life.

When I read the *Record of Joshu*, I feel this acutely. I don't have any personal attachment to living; it would be fine if I died tonight. Zen teaches nonattachment, so I'm not permitted to be attached even to life itself. Every year when I come to America, I do so comfortable with the idea that something could happen along the way and I could die. The senior monks at my monastery know my thinking very well.

But when I read the *Record of Joshu*, I feel like I want to live a long life. It's said Joshu lived to be 120 years old, but I think this is a typical Chinese exaggeration. We can guess he probably lived to be around one hundred years. This March first I turned sixty-nine. But when I read stories about Joshu's life after he was eighty, I feel that even if I can't make it to one hundred, I'd like to live to be at least ninety, because as a Zen master one's Zen mind continues to deepen. If I come back to teach when I'm eighty, someone will tell me, "Roshi, tonight you give a lecture." And I'll reply, "Let's forget about the lecture, and just drink tea." I think that's the state of mind I'd have. When reading the stories in the *Record of Joshu*, I can see what a perfectly complete state of mind Joshu possessed.

22

Zen Teacher, Zen Student: Joshu and Gonyo

The depth of the master's experience allows him to see all of the disciple's experience, whether conscious or unconscious.

THE WAY ZEN MONKS PRACTICED in China in ancient times was to choose one personal master and then travel all around the country visiting different masters, continuing to refine their Zen understanding. A monk would return to his original master after ten or twenty years on the road and become the master's successor. This was the usual way. But in Joshu's case, he didn't leave his master to go on the road, even after this first enlightenment.

The relationship between master and disciple is not just a formal matter of being a good master and being a good disciple. Whether master and disciple are a good fit on a personal basis also matters. I know this from personal experience. I come from a lay family. Rinzai and Soto Zen are both just fine and I could have chosen either, but I happened to choose Rinzai Zen. My family belonged to the Shingon sect, so I did consider becoming a Shingon monk. I happened to know a local Zen master, and because becoming a monk is such a major change of life I went to talk to him about it. He immediately said, "Good. Become my disciple." And I said, "Please." And that's how I became a Zen monk. It would've been fine if I'd remained a Shingon person and became a Shingon monk.

Fortunately I was able to rise in the ranks, so to speak, in the Rinzai sect. If I'd been a Shingon monk, I might still be in the garden sweeping up somewhere. But I entered a Zen monastery at the age of fourteen. That was with my first master. After graduate school, I entered a training monastery and met my second master. So I've had two masters in my life as a monk. Luckily they were both great Zen masters. I was most fortunate to be able to study under these two masters.

In the story of Gonyo Sonja, one of Joshu's Dharma heirs, we find the essence of the teacher-student relationship. Gonyo Sonja brought his mind for his teacher to examine, asking, "After you have thrown everything away in practice, what do you do?" The question itself reveals Gonyo Sonja's serious practice. But it also seems clear that even if all of his worldly desires had disappeared he'd become attached to the idea of his accomplishment. Joshu answered with a single phrase: "Throw it away!"

Even though Gonyo Sonja said he'd thrown it all away, something still bothered him. He had practiced thoroughly, but he was unconsciously sticking to his accomplishment as something. Something remained unfinished; something had not been thrown away. This unfinished business was Gonyo's delusion. In Zen we distinguish between two types of delusion: conscious delusions and unconscious delusions. In the first case you realize your delusion consciously. When you cut a conscious delusion, you realize consciously that you have done so. But unconscious delusions, like Gonyo Sonja's, are delusions that you can't yet see.

Zen teaches complete nonattachment. Joshu could immediately see Gonyo Sonja's sticking point because of the depth of Joshu's practice and the depth of their teacher-student relationship. Whatever's bothering you, throw that away. "Throw it away!" is a very strong teaching, especially at the beginning of practice. Cut it off! Cut it off! Cut it off! This is the practice of nonattachment.

We get to know our attachments through our Zen training, and when we throw them away, we experience the state of nonattachment. One good example of the practice of nonattachment is doing zazen in the rain. If you're sitting in meditation and say, "I can't even hear the sound of the rain," this is not so good. This is actually a state of detachment. Instead, if you hear the sound of the rain and have no problem with either the sound or the rain, this is the experience of nonattachment.

Gonyo Sonja was practicing this nonattachment, and he came to speak to Joshu about it. He didn't understand Joshu's answer, "Throw it away!" so he persisted with another question: "I have no worldly desires, so what on earth do I throw away?" He didn't recognize his attachment to the very idea of his accomplishment—"I have thrown everything away." To this second query, Joshu replied, "Very well then. If you can't throw it away, then keep on carrying it!"

Gonyo's attachment to his belief about what he had accomplished was an unconscious delusion he couldn't see. Joshu, his teacher, helped him to a more thorough view and practice of nonattachment. In order for Gonyo Sonja to be able to let go of the unseen attachment, Joshu first had to help Gonyo to see it. With Joshu's second reply, Gonyo Sonja could see the "it" he was carrying; he could see his unconscious delusion. Now conscious of it, he could throw it away. We can't be free when we are attached; it doesn't matter if the attachment is conscious or unconscious.

This is a good example of how the teacher-disciple relationship functions in Zen. Joshu could see Gonyo's unconscious delusion, even though Gonyo couldn't see it himself. In the experiential training between master and disciple, usually the master has a deeper experience and understanding than the disciple. The depth of the master's experience allows him to see all of the disciple's experience, whether conscious or unconscious. Such was the case for Joshu and Gonyo.

Joshu was truly one of the greatest Zen masters. He traveled from north to south when he was twenty years old to become the student of Master Nansen. It was apparent from an early age that Joshu had something special about him. Joshu practiced with Nansen and, at thirty, he attained great enlightenment. The story of Joshu's enlightenment is very famous. One day, he went to Nansen and asked, "What's the Way of Zen?" Nansen answered, "The mind in daily life is itself the Way." Upon hearing this, Joshu attained great enlightenment. Strictly speaking we should not refer to this as Joshu's first enlightenment experience. Joshu's first enlightenment experience came when he met his teacher.

23

Jiyu: Zen Freedom

You only get half of the goodness of Zen until you understand Joshu's unsurpassable freedom.

THE GREAT TANG DYNASTY Zen master Ummon was quite eloquent. One of his famous sayings was "Every day is a fine day."

How do we interpret "fine"? The fine that Ummon wanted to express is a fine that transcends good and bad; he wasn't just affirming good or bad. We have to deal with nice weather and with rainy days. This is what Ummon meant by fine. He didn't just mean that blue skies are fine days. Many think this is what constitutes a fine day, but don't get too caught up in blue skies. Relate to blue skies freely and freely relate to rainy days. People in the raincoat and umbrella business like rainy days. So it is with good and bad.

When we decide what's good and bad based on egotistical preferences, we believe something's good because it's good for us. These are mistaken values. Nobody lives a completely happy life. Pain and pleasure are fifty-fifty in most lives, so when you encounter pain, just deal with it and go on living. Likewise when you encounter pleasure, just deal with it and go on living. It's okay to cry when you encounter pain. When you encounter pleasure, enjoy it. The world around us is composed entirely of dualistic oppositions. Our practice is to transcend them and live a life of freedom. In this sense, Zen is a path to perfect freedom.

I'd like to explain this notion of freedom. There are two characters in the Japanese word *jiyu*, which is a special Zen term that we usually translate as "freedom." I believe it's better not to translate this word as freedom, but to simply remember it as *jiyu*. The original meaning of the term in ancient China was actually close to the modern meaning of "freedom," but with the advent of Zen in China, many Chinese Zen masters began to use *jiyu* as a special Zen term. So it's important to understand the meaning of the word in the context of Zen.

The problem with translating *jiyu* simply as "freedom" is quite complicated. Chinese characters were in use in Japan even before Buddhism arrived. We Japanese have used Chinese characters in unique and specific ways down through the ages. Then during the Meiji period (late nineteenth to early twentieth century), Western thought, including the Western concept of freedom and liberty, arrived in Japan. At the beginning of the Meiji era, Japanese scholars struggled with how to translate Western terms and concepts into Japanese. One scholar decided to use the characters for *jiyu* to translate the Western concept of freedom and liberty. But this was not quite correct. Although the term *jiyu* had existed in Japan for a long time, aside from Zen monks, few were familiar with it. So when *jiyu* was used to translate the Western notion of freedom and liberty, most Japanese came to understand *jiyu* in this sense, without ever having known the Zen sense of the term. This is why I find it problematic to simply translate *jiyu* as "freedom."

Zen is a religion that is free from attachments. Zen has absolutely no attachments. We come to know our attachments through Zen training. When we throw them away, we experience the state of nonattachment. We cannot be free while we are attached; it doesn't matter whether our attachment is conscious or unconscious. Unconscious delusions are a big problem for mankind. We don't realize that we have these unconscious delusions, and so we act them out over and over again.

Some Zen priests in Japan focus solely on the point of nonattachment. But nonattachment is only really half the story. When asked, "After you have thrown everything away in practice, what do you do?" Joshu replied, "Throw it away!" When his disciple retorted, "I have no worldly desires, so what on earth do I throw away?" Joshu followed with, "Very well then. If you can't throw it away, then keep on carrying it!" We could say that the side of throwing it away and the side of carrying it with us are negative and affirmative sides. *Jiyu*—Zen freedom—comes from being able to hold both the negative and affirmative at the same time. This is why we say Zen is the religion of freedom. This is Joshu's true freedom. This is the freedom Zen teaches. This is the full story.

Because he lives in a state of freedom, Joshu transcends dualistic thinking. He can state the truth affirmatively or negatively. We can directly experience Joshu's attitude and state of mind through his words that transcend the dualism of affirmative and negative. Before the first statement is out of his mouth, the opposite statement appears. His state of mind is such that he freely makes use of both affirmation and denial: sometimes yes, sometimes no. You only get half of the goodness of Zen until you understand Joshu's unsurpassable freedom. This free use of words—expressing truth with the affirmative or with the negative—is a direct expression of Joshu's freedom. When we hear Joshu express this freedom, we have a taste of it ourselves.

The first character in jiyu, *ji*, means "oneself." The second character, *yu*, means "to depend on." Together the term means "to depend on oneself." To depend on oneself sounds egocentric, doesn't it? But *jiyu* is a Buddhist word with special religious meaning. So take care in how you understand "oneself." What kind of "oneself" is it that we can really depend on? The answer in Zen is "the self of Mu."

The Chinese are quite good at coining four-character phrases. For example, by adding the two characters *jizai*, which means "oneself exists," to the term *jiyu* they produce the phrase "oneself is free as one exists." So the Zen meaning of jiyu is positive and quite creative because we're able to act with complete freedom. But this doesn't mean that we're at the center of things acting egotistically. Because we have the essential experience of Mu, our experience of freedom begins with the realization of being Mu. The egotistical side is cut off and we are naturally filled with compassion as we do this. This transformation is an experiential religious conversion. The mind of jiyu or freedom in Zen is also a mind of great compassion and a mind of peace. The ideal way of life, the self of empty mind, is a life of complete freedom. This is the life of enlightenment taught in Zen.

24

Joshu's "Wash Your Bowls"

In Chinese Buddhism, particularly in Zen, teachings are concrete. Here. Now. I myself. What could be more concrete than that?

THE RECORDED STORIES of Zen Master Joshu are really fascinating. There are three volumes, which include a total of 525 stories. In each story, a monk asks Joshu something and Joshu replies. They are a wonderful collection, but Japanese Zen masters rarely lecture on them. There are a couple of reasons for this. For one thing, the most famous stories from the *Record of Joshu* are already included in other collections. Another reason is that with a total of 525 Zen stories, it would take many years to lecture on all of them. I'm in the middle of that process myself right now. In the mid-Edo period (the late eighteenth century), the great Japanese Zen master Hakuin lectured on the *Record of Joshu*. But since then nobody has, until now.

Twenty-two years ago I visited Joshu's temple in China for the first time. Since my visit, it's been rebuilt into a great temple, but twenty years ago it was completely rundown. The wall was collapsing and a tarp was pulled over the chanting hall roof to keep rainwater from leaking in. The temple grounds were covered with grass as tall as a man. But in the middle of the grounds, in the middle of the grass, there was a sixty-foot monolith marking Joshu's tomb. I and a group of twenty priests from my own Tofukuji sect, deeply moved by visiting the great master's final resting place, gathered around Joshu's tomb and chanted. As we chanted, I made a secret promise that during my life as a Zen master, I would lecture on the *Record of Joshu*. I began to fulfill this promise seven years ago. I still have about a hundred stories to go. They're all great stories.

There are many ways to express buddha nature. Some of these I've mentioned before. Zen Master Gutei, for example, would just stick out one finger to show his buddha nature. This is famous as "Gutei's One-Finger Zen." Another Zen master, when asked what the Buddha was, would simply draw a perfect circle in the air. When asked if a dog had buddha nature, of the many different ways to express buddha nature, Joshu simply answered "Mu." The direct translation of *Mu* is "no." This is a difficult aspect of Joshu's answer, because if we simply read the answer intellectually, we may think he meant "No, the dog does not have buddha nature." It isn't the case that Joshu was saying the dog did not have buddha nature. By saying "Mu," Joshu was expressing his very own buddha nature. When Joshu was asked the same question on another occasion, he answered "U," which means "yes." But this "yes" does not in fact mean "Yes, the dog has buddha nature." Sometimes Joshu would say "U" to show his buddha nature.

Both answers—U and Mu, yes and no—express Joshu's buddha nature. There is no problem with U or with Mu. The same applies to the letters A, S, or even Z. Any one will do. Joshu used Mu to respond to the question of whether there is or is not buddha nature; he responded by showing his own buddha nature. Joshu's answer is a real expression of buddha nature. When a Zen monk realizes this point and uses Mu to express his own buddha nature, he doesn't simply say "Mu." He says "MUUUuuuu." In this fashion, the monk tries to show his own buddha nature, and the meaning of the Mu koan.

The full meaning of Joshu's Mu is *Mu bussho*—no buddha nature. During the Tang dynasty when Joshu lived, people elaborated on Joshu's Mu, so it became a koan. Master Mumon Ekai compiled the *Mumonkan* and made Joshu's Mu the first case in that collection. Joshu's Mu has taken on a special meaning and become a very useful Zen training tool. Dokusan always begins with Joshu's Mu koan.

But since Bodhidharma, Zen has been the religion that teaches Mu, regardless of whether Joshu answered Mu or not. Zen is not the religion of Mu because Joshu said "Mu." From its very beginning Zen has been the religion of Mu. Zen is the religion that teaches us to become Mu ourselves. Joshu saying "Mu" in the Tang dynasty was just an accident. But from the Sung dynasty on, Mu became a koan, and you will not solve the koan without yourself becoming Mu.

Master Mumon struggled for six years with the Mu koan. With great pains he asked himself, "What is Mu? What is Mu?" In the end, when he heard the drum in the chanting hall, he was enlightened to Mu. When you hear the *dodom* of the drum, you must become the sound of the drum—*dodom*. This has nothing to do with explanation. When Master Mumon heard the sound *dodom*, Mumon was that sound—*dodom*. To hear the sound is to become the sound. To hear the sound of the drum is to become the sound of the drum. Mumon heard *dodom* and he became *dodom*. This is the essential point of the Mu koan. Having had this experience, Master Mumon put Joshu's Mu koan in the first position when he compiled the *Mumonkan*. Zen Master Mumon provides his own excellent commentaries in *Mumonkan*, which are not at all philosophical. It's a matter of becoming the drum when you hear it. In D. T. Suzuki's words, it is the experience of "transcending dualism."

There's one particularly fine story about an encounter between Joshu and his teacher, Zen Master Nansen. One day Joshu was taking water from a well. Joshu was on the top of the well tower drawing the water up when Master Nansen walked by. One needed a ladder to get to the top of the well tower. Nansen removed the ladder. Joshu saw him do this, and cried out, "Help me! Help me!" Master Nansen and monk Joshu, who was almost a Zen master himself at that point, were simply enjoying each other's Zen experience and depth of Zen mind.

In another story, a newcomer monk showed up one morning and said to Joshu, "I'm a newcomer; I arrived just yesterday. Please give me a teaching suitable to a newcomer." Joshu asked the monk if he'd eaten breakfast, and the monk said he had. Joshu replied, "In that case, go wash your bowls." This is a good teaching. It's an example of the importance of everyday life. All good religions, including Zen, have to teach their followers a way of life. What way of life does Zen teach? Zen teaches how I myself should live here and now. It focuses on here and now, and I myself.

In Chinese Buddhism, particularly in Zen, teachings are concrete. Here. Now. I myself. What could be more concrete than that? "Here, now, I myself" is very important. Once you finish eating breakfast, wash your bowls. "Here" applies to this very situation right now. As a speaker, I myself should here and now concentrate on giving the talk. You, as the listener, should concentrate on listening to it.

This way of life—here, now, I myself—is the focus of Zen.

25

Joshu's "One Tooth"

"I chew my food with just one tooth. A little bit at a time."

That's a good teaching.

THERE IS A STORY about Joshu and a king. Master Rinzai's temple and Master Joshu's temple were in towns relatively close to each other. In ancient times such towns were more like city-states, each with its own king. These kings would go to their local Zen temples to learn Zen. Even the emperor of China learned Zen. Rinzai was a few years older than Joshu, and a young Zen master took over his temple when Rinzai died. The king that lived in the city near Rinzai's temple would normally have gone to study with Rinzai's successor, but he wanted to be instructed by the old Zen master Joshu. So the king traveled south to meet him.

With great respect, he asked Joshu, "You are very old. How many teeth do you have left?"

"Just one," Joshu replied.

The king was shocked and asked, "Just one tooth? How do you chew your food?"

"I chew my food with just one tooth. A little bit at a time."

That's a good teaching. You can see the concrete "here, now, and I myself" in it. If you have only five teeth, live with just five teeth. If you have only three teeth left, live with just three teeth.

These days few people get a chance to experience just one tooth. Last year I had some dental problems. There are many great dentists out there and I went to a dentist who is also a friend. I hadn't visited a dentist for a long time. He said, "You know, Head Abbot, I'm sure you're very busy, but you really ought to come see me more often." He checked my teeth and said, "We're going to have to pull three teeth." I was shocked. In Japan if you have to have three teeth pulled, they pull one tooth per week. But my dentist said he was pulling all three teeth that day. Even his young nurse was concerned and whispered to him, "Doctor, you're pulling all three teeth at once?"

"Don't worry," my good friend, the dentist, replied, "This head abbot is a Zen master." I myself was worried, but they pulled all three teeth anyway. Ow! It was very painful, but as I endured the pain, the story of Joshu and his one tooth was rattling around in my brain. These days we don't have to live with just one tooth, but Joshu's teaching—chew your food with just one tooth—continues to be relevant. Our lives are filled with many different situations, but no matter the situation, we should live our lives responding appropriately and freely.

On one of the yearly visits to China that I lead for the monks of Tofukuji we went to a rural village, not for sightseeing but because in ancient times there had been an important temple there. The temple had long since disappeared, but we decided to visit the village anyway. The head of the village was thrilled to receive us and wanted to do something to welcome us. The village was so remote and rural that no foreign priest had ever visited before, and because the village was so poor they had no way to greet us properly. There was, however, a skilled old calligrapher in the village. It was decided that he would welcome us.

When we arrived at the village entrance, the head of the village greeted us and apologized for not being able to offer us a proper welcome ceremony, explaining that instead the old calligrapher would give a demonstration of calligraphy. I imagined the demonstration would take place in some kind of hall, but it was to take place outside. When we arrived at the appointed location, the calligrapher was propping up the legs of a rickety old table with rocks in the middle of a field. The thirty of us surrounded the table and said hello in Chinese. Once the table was made sturdy enough to keep it from falling over, the old calligrapher took a crumpled wad of paper out of his pocket, flattened it out, and began to grind his ink on an ink stone.

This old calligrapher from the great country of China was taking his time. When we looked closely we saw there was old leftover ink on his stone. He added water and began grinding the old ink. In Japanese calligraphy you really are supposed to use ink the same day that it's been ground, but the old calligrapher didn't care and began grinding the old coagulated ink. We Japanese priests looked at each other, wondering, "He's going to write with *that*?!"

The old calligrapher had only one brush; it was quite thin, and its tip was caked with ink. When you finish writing calligraphy for the day, you must rinse the tip of your brush with water, but it appeared that this fellow had never washed his brush. It was thoroughly caked. In the old days in Japan, they'd clean their brushes, and if a brush was caked with ink you'd bite it to soften the bristles. Then, once it was softened up, you could begin writing. When the old calligrapher bit his brush, the Zen priest standing next to me whispered, "Roshi, he only has one tooth." Having only one tooth, it took him a long time to soften the brush, but I thought it was a great opportunity, so I asked all the Tofukuji priests if they'd ever heard the story of Joshu and his one tooth. They hadn't, so I told it to them while the old calligrapher chewed on his brush. As a result, all the priests with me on the trip now know the story of Joshu and his one tooth.

At last, the old calligrapher finished chewing and softening the tip of his brush. He dipped it in the coagulated ink. When we do calligraphy, we hold the brush at a particular angle, but in China they hold it differently. The old guy began to write a famous poem from the Tang dynasty. His calligraphy was excellent! All thirty of us applauded.

If you have only one tooth, chew your brush with only one tooth. This is the way of life—here, now, I myself—that Zen teaches.

26

Joshu's Playful Zen

Joshu's reply to the monk used the words of a playful children's song. This was Joshu's way of telling the monk to have more fun, to play more.

YOU'RE BOUND TO COME ACROSS stories of rough or extreme behavior when you read about Tang dynasty Zen masters. Sometimes people misunderstand and equate that kind of behavior with the attainment of satori enlightenment. Shibayama Roshi always severely criticized such behavior. The number of such Zen masters has declined in my generation, but during my master Shibayama's lifetime, such rough Zen masters still existed. One, in particular, was a big drinker. In Japan many Buddhist priests drink alcohol. I think this is a problem. The fifth basic Buddhist precept says not to drink alcohol, but Japanese Buddhists interpret the commandments more broadly. I myself don't drink alcohol. Once I said that I intend to give a lecture on the issue of drinking among priests, and five priests from Tofukuji sect subtemples grabbed my sleeve and pleaded, "No, Master, please don't!" But I promise that I will do it when I turn eighty.

There is some benefit in interpreting Buddhist precepts broadly. We could interpret the fifth precept to mean "don't drink too much" or "don't drink excessively." One master during Shibayama Roshi's time loved to drink and was always drunk. Nowadays there are no trolleys in Kyoto, but there used to be. This Zen master laid down across the tracks in the middle of the street and said, "I'll stop the trolleys!" This is also one of the Mu koans. He did this when the trolleys had already shut down for the night, but the story blew up in the news. Shibayama Roshi was really mad about it; that master was just aping the rough behavior of Tang dynasty masters. The next day when he'd sobered up, he reflected on his actions. If he hadn't, we couldn't call him a Zen master.

There is a mountain in India that resembles an eagle, called Vulture Peak, which is where the Buddha taught what we know as the *Lotus Sutra*. Once on Vulture Peak, Buddha held up a flower and his disciple Kasho, upon seeing it, began to laugh. The Buddha said that this is how he passed his teaching and understanding on to Kasho. We consider this to be the beginning of Zen, a teaching that places great emphasis on actual experience, with letters and words being of secondary importance. Buddha taught from his heart, just by holding up a flower. If you have true Zen experience, you can understand this teaching. In Zen one teaches with one's heart, going beyond words. People with deep Zen understanding and experience can relate without words. Buddha's disciple Kasho had reached the same satori—the same level of spiritual understanding—as Buddha. In Zen the disciple must understand the master's or teacher's mind directly. This is how Zen was transmitted first from Shakyamuni Buddha to his disciple Kasho and so on thereafter, from one successor to another down through the ages.

In story 444 in the *Record of Joshu*, when a monk arrives to meet Joshu, he asks him, "Where are you from?" The monk answers, "I come from the South." Most Zen monks at that time lived in the south of China near the Yangtze River, but Joshu lived in the north by the Yellow River. Nowadays, we can look things up quite easily, but of course there was no internet in Tang dynasty China. So how did they get information? Monks would meet when traveling around the country and one would say to the other, "Hey! You've got to go meet Zen Master Joshu. He's up north by the Yellow River." Many monks traveled from the south to meet Zen Master Joshu.

We can be sure that the monk would have been nervous about meeting the great Zen master Joshu when he replied, "I come from the South." Wanting to put him at ease a bit, Joshu said, "Don't say something so silly after traveling so far." The monk hadn't actually said anything silly, but this is how Joshu replied. The monk, having been quite earnest in his initial answer, said, "I've never said anything silly in my whole life!"

How did the great master Joshu respond? Before I translate his response, I should note that it was in Chinese. I never studied Chinese, so this is merely my imitation Chinese. Joshu said in a sing-song voice, "*Chii-yan-ka. Chii-yan-ka.*" *Chii* means to hold or catch, *yan* means a willow tree, and *ka* means flowers. There are many willow trees in China and in springtime the petals of the willow blossoms float around in the air like snow. Chinese kids run around trying to catch the floating petals, singing, "*Chii-yan-ka. Chii-yan-ka.*" So Joshu's reply to the monk used the words of a playful children's song. This was Joshu's way of telling the monk to have more fun, to play more. When commenting on this story, it's appropriate to act like a child chasing blossoms, and not to rely on just words alone to express Joshu's teaching.

It's perfectly fine for an enlightened person to act normally. The idea that attaining satori enlightenment makes you strange or abnormal is wrong. Today, in both Japan and the West, some imagine that Zen can make you a superman. I've been practicing and training in Zen since I was fourteen, and now I'm a Zen master and the head of a Zen sect. The fact is there's nothing spectacular about people who've attained satori. In the winter it's cold for us and in the summer it's hot. When we're sad, we cry. When we're happy, we're happy with everyone. And when someone is in trouble, out of compassion we act for him or her without a second thought. There's no special mind, no special state.

"East Mountain Walks on Water"

Calligraphy by Keido Fukushima

IV.

Classical Teaching Stories

27

Bodhidharma's Zen

Bodhidharma wanted to help the emperor understand that to really know, one must transcend
knowing and not knowing.

BODHIDHARMA WAS ORIGINALLY from India, the twenty-eighth
Buddhist Patriarch in a lineage stretching back to Shakyamuni
Buddha. He was originally the prince of a kingdom in South India.
One day, Hannyatara,[2] the twenty-seventh Patriarch, arrived in the
kingdom, and Bodhidharma's father presented Hannyatara with a
beautiful jewel. According to the historical record, it was referred to
as the most valuable jewel in the world, a priceless treasure. Upon
receiving it, Hannyatara asked the three princes of the kingdom,
"This is a precious jewel, but is it the most precious jewel in the
world?" The two older princes both said that it was, that there was
no jewel more precious. But the third prince, Bodhidharma, said,
"The mind that perceives this jewel as being the most precious, that
mind itself is even more precious." Hannyatara was delighted with
this answer and asked the king's permission to make Bodhidharma
his disciple. Of course, this story is a fabrication written long after
Bodhidharma's era.

Bodhidharma is known as the person who brought Zen to
China. But what exactly did he transmit to China? It was the mind
of Zen. The story of his meeting with Hannyatara when he was a

young prince was invented to support this transmission. Be that as it may, Bodhidharma did become Hannyatara's disciple and after completing his training became his successor. It was Hannyatara who ordered him to go to China. There are so few historical sources related to Bodhidharma that for a time many scholars believed he never really existed. However his existence is generally accepted these days, although he may be a representation of several historical figures. In any case, Bodhidharma traveled from India to China. There are two theories about how he got there. According to one theory he crossed the mountains of Tibet en route to China. According to the second he traveled to China by sea. This second theory is the more commonly accepted of the two.

When Bodhidharma arrived, China was divided into three kingdoms, the southernmost of which was called Ryo. In the capital, Nanking, Bodhidharma met with the emperor of Ryo. The emperor's name was Butei. The character for *Bu* in his name means fighting. In Chinese history there are four famous emperors named Bu. Three of them suppressed Buddhism; only Emperor Butei of Ryo supported Buddhism. He'd been a Taoist for a time but converted to Buddhism. He studied Buddhism in depth, translated sutras, and wrote commentaries on them. He built many great temples, invited many monks and nuns to his palace, and made donations to them. According to the beliefs of his day, he had performed many good deeds in support of Buddhism.

When Bodhidharma came to see him, the emperor asked, "Since I've done so many good deeds, will there be any merit for me in this life or the next?" Bodhidharma answered *"Muku doku,"* which, translated literally, means "no merit." You must be careful when you come across Zen expressions that appear to be negative like this one. *Mu,* the first character of the phrase *muku doku,* is negative, but the expression itself does not simply mean that there's no merit. What

Bodhidharma intended to communicate was that one should not hope for merit from doing good deeds. Instead, truly great deeds are performed without attachment or hope for reward.

The Zen that Bodhidharma transmitted to China teaches us to act out of nonattachment. Please don't misunderstand the meaning of nonattachment. Zen talks about nonattachment, but it's not a simple matter. When your ego gets wrapped up with your desires, they become delusions. You need to keep this in mind in trying to understand the meaning of *muku doku*, "No merit"—Bodhidharma's first teaching in China.

Emperor Butei was probably rather confused by Bodhidharma's "No merit," and so he went on to ask a second question of a more scholarly nature: "Is there such a thing as the holy satori enlightenment of Buddhism?" Bodhidharma responded, *"Kakunen musho."* This is another phrase with which it is important to be careful. The first word, *kakunen*, means "vast emptiness," and refers to a perfectly blue sky without a single cloud in it. The second word, *musho*, which literally means "not holy," is the most important part of the phrase. *Mu* in *musho* is again negative. But we must interpret its meaning with great care. Bodhidharma wasn't simply saying there's nothing holy. He intended to communicate that real holiness transcends both holy and not holy. His teaching was concerned with transcending dualism. So his first teaching was about nonattachment and his second was about transcending dualistic oppositions.

The emperor basically gave up with Bodhidharma's "Vast emptiness, nothing holy," so his third question revealed that he was a bit upset. "You just told me there's nothing holy," the emperor said, "but what about you? Aren't you an enlightened and, therefore, holy person?" Bodhidharma answered, *"Fushiki,"* which literally means "I don't know." The *fu* of *fushiki* is negative. By saying "I don't know,"

Bodhidharma wanted to help the emperor understand that to really know, one must transcend knowing and not knowing.

Bodhidharma offered three teachings upon his arrival in China. The first was "No merit," *muku doku*, the second was "Vast emptiness, nothing holy," *kakunen musho*, and the third was "I don't know," *fushiki*. These three teachings contain Zen's essence— nonattachment and transcending dualism. These are two of the pillars of Zen Buddhism. Unfortunately Emperor Butei was not able to understand Bodhidharma's teaching, nor could many Chinese Buddhist monks of the time understand it. What's more, a group of extreme Chinese monks felt that Bodhidharma's weird brand of Buddhism was dangerous and they tried to poison him. There is a painting of Bodhidharma in which he's missing the teeth on one side of his mouth. This is to show that he lost his teeth as a result of being poisoned. He knew if he remained in Ryo, he'd be killed, so he fled north crossing the Yangtze River. Bodhidharma's flight north is a popular motif in paintings in which he's shown crossing the Yangtze on a single leaf. Some people imagine Bodhidharma had special powers that allowed him to cross in such a fashion, but the leaf is just a symbolic way to show that he crossed in a tiny boat.

Bodhidharma continued to the north and arrived at Shaolin Temple. Shaolin Temple is where kung fu originated. Bodhidharma, concluding that China was not yet ready for Zen, took up residence in a nearby cave, where he began to meditate. Fortunately, one day a Chinese monk named Eka came to him. If Eka hadn't come to see him, the development of Zen in China would have been delayed. Eka became a monk very early in his life. He was a diligent student and traveled throughout China in pursuit of spiritual training, but never attained enlightenment. Finally he came to Bodhidharma and asked to be his disciple. Bodhidharma initially refused to answer. According to the record, this took place in January, the coldest time of the year in this part of China. Eka's wish to become Bodhidharma's disciple was so strong that he stood outside Bodhidharma's cave all night long. There was a snowstorm that night.

The following morning Bodhidharma asked, "You've been standing out in the snow all night. What do you want?"

"Out of great compassion, please teach me, Master!" Eka replied.

"The practice of Zen is not such an easy matter," Bodhidharma said. "If you really want to get enlightenment, you must be willing to sacrifice your life."

Chinese monks in those days used to carry small knives. At Bodhidharma's reply, Eka pulled out his knife, cut off his left arm, and placed it before Bodhidharma to show he was willing to sacrifice his life to practice. Bodhidharma accepted him as a disciple.

"I've been practicing for so long," Eka said, "but my mind is still not at ease. Please put my mind at ease."

"Bring me your mind and I'll put it at ease." Bodhidharma replied.

Eventually, Eka came up with a good response, but it's not clear how long it took Eka to come up with it when you read the record. Having completed Zen training myself, I know that Eka's response was not easily arrived at. Eka's eventual response was, "I've been looking for my mind, but in the end, I couldn't find it." The first Chinese character of Eka's response means "in the end," which makes it clear that he had been working on the matter for a very long time before he realized it was impossible to grasp the mind. The mind is not to be found anywhere. The expression "I cannot find my mind" is very important.

Hearing Eka's response, Bodhidharma said, "There, your mind is at ease."

The whole Buddhist religion began with Shakyamuni Buddha's awakening. The essence of his awakening was that nothing has permanent self-nature, that everything is empty. Eka's answer, "I cannot find my mind," expresses the very same understanding in a Chinese way, more concretely and less philosophically. You cannot find your mind. It's impossible because the mind is empty. Simply realizing this fact in itself puts the mind at ease.

Realizing this emptiness is called "the mind of Mu." When your mind is empty, you can't find it anywhere. When your mind is empty, you can interact with life freely. You can receive whatever comes your way with complete freedom. Thus the mind of Mu is also a free mind: each moment is creative and fresh. Because your mind is empty, you can't find it, and realizing the mind that can't be found is itself satori enlightenment. When Eka said he couldn't find his mind, he'd awakened to this. When Bodhidharma said "Your mind is at ease," he was acknowledging Eka's enlightenment.

28

The Sixth Ancestor: Buddhism Becomes Zen

To say that there is a pure body of satori enlightenment or a mind resembling a polished mirror reveals
a final attachment from the perspective of Mu.

IT WAS THE SIXTH PATRIARCH, Eno, who really made Buddhism into Chinese Zen. Eno was born in the region of Canton in southern China. It's fair to say that Eno was a religious genius. As a layman, he had to work to support his mother, which he did by chopping wood and selling firewood. From the beginning, Eno was possessed of a kind of Buddhist spark. One day while he was out selling firewood, he heard a monk chanting the *Diamond Sutra*. Of course, being an illiterate layperson, Eno didn't recognize it as the *Diamond Sutra*. An important line appears in the sutra that states that the original mind shines forth when there's nowhere to dwell. Eno was deeply moved when he heard the monk chant this line.

He asked the monk what he was reciting, and the monk told him it was the *Diamond Sutra*. When asked where he had learned the sutra, the monk replied that he learned it in a place near the Yangtze River where the Fifth Patriarch was teaching Zen. Eno immediately wanted to meet the Fifth Patriarch. First he provided means for his mother to live, then he set out to meet the Fifth Patriarch. Eno's religious mind is apparent in the way he thought about and cared for his mother. You can't be considered a truly religious or spiritual person if you don't care for your parents.

When Eno finally reached the Fifth Patriarch, the Patriarch asked him where he came from. Eno answered that he'd come from the south. When asked what he was looking for, Eno said he wanted to become a buddha. The Fifth Patriarch replied that people from the south have no buddha nature so they can't become buddhas. The *Nirvana Sutra* famously says that all beings have primary buddha nature, which the Fifth Patriarch of course knew. But he was constantly challenging his disciples and this was how he challenged Eno. Without knowing the *Nirvana Sutra*, Eno replied, "Indeed, there are north and south, but there's no north and south when it comes to buddha nature. So I too can become Buddha." Eno may have been a layperson, but this was a good answer and the Fifth Patriarch allowed Eno to enter the temple.

In those days when a layperson wanted to become a monk, he would enter a temple hall known as the Hall for Election of Monks. He would train in that hall for a period of time before becoming a monk, then he would shave his head and enter the Hall for Election of Buddhas as a monk. There were always two such halls in big monasteries. Many Buddhist temples and big monasteries have been rebuilt with two such halls since the end of the Cultural Revolution.

Although Eno was admitted to the Hall for Election of Monks, his work at the monastery was threshing rice. Even so, Eno was actually doing Buddhist practice during this time. One day the Fifth Patriarch decided it was time to choose his successor and instructed all his monks to express their Zen state of mind in a poem. The best of the monks was named Jinshu. All the other monks assumed Jinshu would be the Fifth Patriarch's successor. Even if they composed their own poems, they assumed they wouldn't be able to match him. Jinshu published his poem, which is now a very famous four-line poem. The first line says one's body is like the tree of enlightenment and the second line says that one's mind is like a pure mirror—in other words, both body and mind are pure. The third line says that although they're pure, they must always be polished, and the fourth line says that this is done to keep dust from settling. It's a pretty good poem. The third and fourth lines express the need for effort in practice to keep one's mind clear of illusions. All the monks appreciated the poem as a show of how accomplished in Zen Jinshu was.

But Eno, working in the barn threshing rice, was not so impressed. He thought Jinshu's poem wasn't penetrating enough, so he wrote a four-line poem of his own. The first line read, "There is no such thing as the tree of enlightenment," the second read, "nor is there such a thing as a pure mirror," the third read, "Originally, there's not a single thing," and the fourth line read, "So where could a speck of dust settle?"

If you have some Zen understanding and compare these two poems, you can see that Eno's poem is a penetrating expression of Zen mind. The third line is the most important. "Originally, there's not a single thing." This is an expression original to Eno. If I had to express all of Buddhist teaching in one word, that word would be *shunyata* (Sanskrit) or *ku* (Japanese), which means "emptiness." In China through the influence of Taoism, this concept of emptiness was expressed with the character *Mu*. Eno's expression—that originally there is not a single thing—is really an expression of Mu. To say that there is a pure body of satori enlightenment or a mind resembling a polished mirror reveals a final attachment from the perspective of Mu. It is not true penetration into *ku*, emptiness. Eno's statement is free of attachment. It completely penetrates Mu.

Some theorize that both poems were actually composed later. Jinshu eventually became a Zen master in northern China and Eno became a Zen master in southern China. According to the story, the Fifth Patriarch judged the poems, said Eno's was superior, and decided to make Eno the Sixth Patriarch. But Eno was still a layperson; he had not yet entered the second Hall for Election of Buddhas. If the Fifth Patriarch made this decision public, hundreds of his disciples might be offended. The Fifth Patriarch was a realist; there could be some danger to Eno. So during the night, the Fifth Patriarch found Eno where he was threshing rice and told him he wanted to transmit the Dharma to him and give him the robe and bowl that had been handed down from Bodhidharma. The robe and bowl are symbols of transmission. He also told Eno he must flee and escape to the south.

The *Platform Sutra* of the Sixth Patriarch includes many details of what happened that night: Eno said he didn't know where to find a boat to escape across the river to the south; the Fifth Patriarch said he'd accompany him; they got on a boat, and the Fifth Patriarch rowed; Eno said that it wasn't good for the master to do the rowing and that the disciple should be the one to row; the Fifth Patriarch said because he was the master he should row the disciple across to the other shore; and Eno pointed out that he had already received Dharma transmission, so he himself could teach—in other words, he himself could also row the boat. Of course these are symbolic expressions. In the Zen tradition a master must be very careful about producing a successor. That's what this exchange is about. In any case Eno thanked his master from his heart and headed south.

29

The Sixth Ancestor Becomes a Teacher

In both Japan and America, people have misunderstood Zen as something mystical, but this is untrue. There are no secrets in Zen. Zen dislikes secrets because Zen is here, now, I myself, so there's nothing to be hidden.

AFTER HE TRANSMITTED the Dharma to Eno, the Fifth Patriarch didn't give a lecture for three days. His seven hundred disciples wondered if he was sick. Explaining that he was not sick and that he'd already transmitted the Dharma, the Fifth Patriarch said he was finished teaching. When his disciples asked him to whom he had transmitted it, he told them it was to Eno, the monk who'd been threshing rice at the monastery. His disciples were shocked. One of them, Myozoja (also known as Emo), who had been a general before becoming a monk, was quite angry. He decided to pursue Eno to retrieve the robe and bowl.

Eno, now the Sixth Patriarch of Zen, had a three-day head start, but Myozoja caught up with him on Daiyu Peak—one of the five peaks where there is a memorial rock. Myozoja demanded that Eno return the robe and bowl. Eno placed them on the memorial rock, but Myozoja could not move them. The robe and the bowl are objects that one relates to with one's Zen mind rather than with physical strength. Myozoja had experience practicing Zen, so he realized that it had been a mistake to try to take the robe and bowl from Eno. In the record it says the robe and bowl were immovable. But a robe and bowl are not so heavy; they were immovable because Myozoja realized his mistake.

Myozoja politely said to Eno, "You've provided me with a secret meaning. Please teach me further."

In response, Eno offered his first teaching: "Don't think good, don't think bad. At that very moment, what is your true self?"

This expression, "Don't think good, don't think bad," is very important. Zen is the religion that teaches Mu. You cannot really translate Mu. Translated literally, it means "nothing" or "nonexistence." But in Zen, Mu includes notions such as "things aren't while they are, and they are while they're not." Earlier, I said the Indian concept of *shunyata*—emptiness—became Mu in China. The line "Form is emptiness and emptiness is form" from the *Heart Sutra* addresses this. It means it is but it's not, it's not but it is. This is difficult to grasp philosophically, but if you don't understand this point, you don't understand Buddhism. In Zen, such notions are included in Mu.

Zen emphasizes experience, and experience is an individual matter. If someone else experiences something, the experience is theirs, not yours. You must have your own experience. Zen questions the self. A teaching that doesn't question the self isn't Zen. There is no point in just saying "here and now" without "I myself." You must include the self. This is what Eno meant by "What is your true self?"—the second part of this teaching on Daiyu Peak. When Eno asked this question, Myozoja became enlightened and began to cry. He thanked Eno and asked that if there was an additional secret teaching, an even deeper teaching, would Eno please share it. "In Zen there are no secrets." Eno said, "If there is a secret, it must be yours."

Nothing is hidden in Zen. In both Japan and America, people have misunderstood Zen as something mystical, but this is untrue. There are no secrets in Zen. Zen dislikes secrets because Zen is here, now, I myself, so there's nothing to be hidden.

We don't know where Eno spent the next fifteen years after the exchange on the mountain. As I have mentioned, Eno was a genius. He received Dharma transmission when he was quite young. Even though he was the Sixth Patriarch, he didn't immediately assume the role. He spent fifteen years in the mountains deepening his practice. This is important. In Zen we call this "special practice." Finally, at the age of thirty-nine, he appeared for the first time as the Sixth Patriarch at the temple Hasshoji in Canton. Eno hadn't yet shaved his head; there's a painting in which you can see him with long hair. When Eno arrived the resident priest of Hasshoji was giving a lecture before a large audience of monks. In those days a flag was raised outside the temple when a lecture was scheduled. On this particular occasion the flag was waving in the wind. One of the monks said, "The flag is moving." Another said, "No, it's the wind that's moving." And they went on to have a heated discussion without reaching any agreement on the matter. Eno overheard the discussion and remarked, "It's not the wind that moves, and it's not the flag. It's your mind that moves." This is a Zen teaching that questions the self. It was Eno's second sermon.

Hearing Eno's comment, the resident priest of the temple said, "Someone who can teach like this must be the Sixth Patriarch." Eno acknowledged that indeed he was. Eno shaved his head at Hasshoji for the first time, and his hair is preserved in the pagoda there.

30

Baso and the Self

When someone asked Master Baso "What is Zen?"
he answered, "My own mind (or heart), just as it is,
is Buddha."

ZEN MASTER BASO had a disciple named Hyakujo. The story of
Hyakujo's first satori experience is quite famous. Hyakujo was walking with Baso through a meadow. They saw some wild geese taking
off. Baso asked, "What are they?" and Hyakujo replied, "Wild geese."
Baso continued, "Where did they go?" and Hyakujo answered, "They
flew away." Baso gave Hyakujo's nose a tweak, Hyakujo howled, and
Baso said, "They haven't gone anywhere." At this point Hyakujo had
a realization.

This story has an important Zen meaning. If something has no
relationship to you yourself, it's not Zen. We could call Zen the religion that teaches the self and its relationship to everything. Most people these days don't really know themselves very well. The English
historian Arnold Toynbee once said that modern people know many
things, but they don't know themselves. He said this long ago, but
it's still the case. Modern people are quite intellectual and know a
great deal, but they really don't know themselves. If you put aside the
question of your self, you cannot really speak about Zen.

If you are doing koan study and try to do dokusan by telephone
and via phone you say, "I have become the mountain," that's only

an explanation. The experience of becoming the mountain lives in a completely different dimension. When Zen asks for the *self*, we're speaking about an experience. In Zen teaching, we say, "When you see a mountain, become the mountain; when you walk along a river, become the river." In the Zen records when you find expressions like seeing, knowing, or hearing, you should understand them as becoming. If you do so, your understanding of Zen will deepen. This advice will be useful for those of you who participate in dokusan.

In Zen, it's fundamentally a question of becoming the self. You won't find this in the Zen records, but you could say Zen is the religion of self-becoming. In the dialogue between Master Baso and Hyakujo concerning the flying geese, Master Baso asked, "What are they?" This is a good Zen question. If Hyakujo already had deep Zen understanding, he wouldn't have simply said, "They are wild geese." I think he would more likely have become a wild goose. But in this case he did not. Out of compassion Baso asked Hyakujo where the geese went. Again, Hyakujo should have had some realization. If he had, he would have given a good answer, something like "They didn't go anywhere. Here I am." That would have been a good Zen answer. But Hyakujo simply said they had gone. Master Baso saw that Hyakujo still didn't understand, so he twisted his nose, by which he was really asking, "What is this self here?"

When Baso twisted Hyakujo's nose, Hyakujo had his first Zen experience, but he continued to train. Several years later, he and Baso had a conversation involving a *hossu*—a stick with what looks like a long horse's tail attached at one end. Its original purpose was to chase away mosquitos, but over time it became the habit of Zen masters to hold a *hossu* when teaching. So the *hossu* became a symbol of a Zen master. Zen Master Baso and Hyakujo were discussing the *hossu* when Baso gave a great Zen shout—a *katsu*! He shouted this out with a great voice. In Zen this cry of *katsu* is something important. Hearing Baso's *katsu* Hyakujo finally reached great enlightenment.

Hyakujo eventually became a Zen master himself and told this story to his own successor, Obaku. Obaku was the master of Rinzai, who founded the Rinzai sect. In any case, Hyakujo told Obaku about how he had studied under Baso and finally reached great enlightenment when he heard Baso's *katsu*. He said that he couldn't hear for three days afterward. This shows just how great Baso's *katsu* really was.

So in Zen only the *self* is the focus. That's what Master Baso wanted to teach. Hyakujo, his nose twisted, crying out in pain, had his first Zen realization. Baso's teaching was a fine teaching. There are many stories about Master Baso, who was called "Great Master Baso," in the *Mumonkan*—an indication of what a truly wonderful master he was.

In another famous story, when someone asked Master Baso "What is Zen?" he answered, "My own mind (or heart), just as it is, is Buddha." The four-character Chinese phrase that expresses this is read as *soku shin, soku butsu* in Japanese. This is an example of Master Baso's creative expression and something he employed as a skillful teaching. Master Baso had four or five hundred young monks studying under him. During Baso's time in China, there was no special, fixed time for Zen question-and-answer sessions. When two monks met in the street, they would simply enter into dialogue. The greeting itself would begin the dialogue. In one case a young monk who didn't really understand the meaning of Baso's *soku shin, soku butsu* just imitated it. It was fashionable for young monks in those days to do this. So in his later years, Master Baso began to express the opposite teaching, which, when translated literally, means, "what is not mind, not heart, is not Buddha." This is a negation of his previous teaching. Because monks had become too attached to his previous teaching, Master Baso denied his original statement. This is further evidence of what a great master Baso was.

Daibai ("Big Plum"), one of Baso's disciples, had a very deep practice. After finishing his training with Baso he went alone into the mountains to continue training and to deepen his realization. Knowing this and interested in seeing how far Daibai had developed, Baso sent another disciple to check on Daibai. When the disciple found him, Daibai asked, "What teaching does our master offer these days?" The disciple told him that Baso no longer used the expression "My own mind, just as it is, is Buddha" but had instead taken to saying the opposite. Upon hearing this, Daibai said, "Master Baso can say the opposite all he likes, but I'll stick with 'My own mind, just as it is, is Buddha.'" Upon returning to Baso, the young monk told him about his conversation with Daibai. When Master Baso heard Daibai's retort, he said "This Big Plum has ripened!" This is great praise, indeed.

Later another of Master Baso's excellent disciples, a layman by the name of Mr. Ho, heard that a big plum had ripened. He decided to go to the mountain and see for himself. Mr. Ho found Daibai in the mountains. The two of them had trained under Master Baso together and so were already good friends.

"How ripe has the plum become?" Mr. Ho asked Daibai.

"Please taste it," Daibai replied.

Mr. Ho said, "I'll chew you up!"

"Please, at least leave me the pit!" Daibai replied.

The story of Mr. Ho and Daibai is one of the most famous of the many stories in the history of Zen that involve laypeople. Zen Master Baso was a great teacher and both Mr. Ho and Daibai can be considered great successors.

31

Hyakujo's Fox and Transcending Duality

We must transcend the two sides: the side of being
bound by cause and effect and the side of not being
bound by it.

MASTER HYAKUJO DEVELOPED into a master who was able to
stand up to his own great master, Baso. Hyakujo's name literally
means "a hundred meters." Daiyuzan, the mountain where Hyakujo
lived, was nicknamed Hyakujo for its height, 100 meters, and
Hyakujo came to be known in association with the mountain where
he lived. One day a monk asked Hyakujo, "What's the most excellent
thing in Zen?" Hyakujo replied, "I sit alone on Mount Daiyuzan."
This is a famous line, as is Hyakujo's famous teaching, "A day without work is a day without food."

Hyakujo provided some great teachings that live on. The second
case of the *Mumonkan*, called the Fox Koan, is another example of
his teaching. The story, you must understand, is just a made-up story
based on the Eastern view of the fox as a trickster. The story deals
with the question of cause and effect.

The concept of cause and effect was developed in Indian Buddhism. Even today American students ask me about cause and effect
and reincarnation. The idea of reincarnation comes up in Indian
Buddhism as the belief that something good will happen in the next
life if you do good in this life, and that there will likewise be bad

consequences in the next life if you do bad in this life. This is the theory of cause and effect. But the teaching that what happens in this world affects what happens in the next world isn't real. Only this life is important for us humans. We have to wholeheartedly live this life. In Buddhism we believe in those who wholeheartedly live this life. As for what past, present, and future are, we would simply answer yesterday, today, and tomorrow. This is the Zen way of thinking: just this life itself, this "self-becoming" that really exists.

The second case in the *Mumonkan* is an example of this teaching. Whenever Hyakujo gave a *teisho*, a Dharma talk, an old layman attended, listening with the monks and leaving with them when the lecture ended. One day the old man remained behind and spoke with Master Hyakujo. He began by saying, "I'm not actually a human being. I'm a fox." There is an old idea that originated in China that foxes are able to change their appearance. The Japanese have shared this belief for a long time. They believe foxes play tricks on human beings. When the old man stayed behind to tell Hyakujo he wasn't human, he went on to say that he used to be a human being, five hundred human lives before, when he was himself the resident priest of that very temple. At the time, he explained, a monk in training asked him if a human being is subject to the law of cause and effect. "No," he had answered, "humans are not subject to it." Due to that answer, he was transformed into a fox and lived as a fox for five hundred lifetimes. But he wanted to resume his human life and so went to visit the new priest on Mount Hyakujo. Hyakujo, being the new priest, suggested the old man ask him the same question the young training monk had asked five hundred years before. And so the old man asked, "Am I bound by cause and effect or not?" "Yes," Hyakujo answered, "one has a relationship to cause and effect."[3] Hearing this, the fox was able resume life as a human.

Now, keep in mind that this story is something Hyakujo made up to teach about cause and effect. We must wholeheartedly live this life. It is our Zen way of thinking that only this life really exists. Hyakujo invented this story about past lives and the fox because the Chinese in Hyakujo's time believed such things. Why had the old man been changed into a fox? Because the theory of cause and effect has a human dimension to it.

Hyakujo's disciples didn't really understand the meaning of what transpired in the story, so Hyakujo invited them to follow him around to the back of the temple. He said they would find the corpse of a recently deceased fox. The monks did find it and held a monk's funeral service for it. What was Hyakujo trying to teach? Even though we've had the law of cause and effect since the time of Indian Buddhism, you must not be bound by it. Hyakujo wanted to teach us that we must transcend the two sides: the side of being bound by cause and effect and the side of not being bound by it.

Of course there is cause and effect in the real world. The fact that we were born into this world is due to our parents; they were our cause and we are the effect. We can't deny it. Still from the standpoint of Zen, it's not good to be bound by cause and effect. Zen teaches an intimate relationship with oneself, but this doesn't mean being driven by cause and effect. You must be the subject that uses cause and effect. Hyakujo was teaching us to be masters who freely use cause and effect. The old master became a fox because he said humans were not bound by cause and effect, but Hyakujo said the opposite, affirming cause and effect and returning the fox to human form. Hyakujo taught that we have to throw away our attachment to cause and effect. This is the point of the second case in the *Mumonkan*. We shouldn't be bound by cause and effect; we should become capable of freely using cause and effect.

32

Master Bokuju Trains Ummon

Bokuju would open the door a little wider, grab the
monk by his collar, shake him hard, push him down,
and say, "This fellow had no purpose whatsoever."

ZEN MASTER UMMON lived in China at the end of the Tang
dynasty. He had his leg very badly broken in training with Bokuju.
Master Bokuju was rather strange. It was he who enabled both Rinzai
and Ummon to gain satori enlightenment. I'm not sure whether it
is quite appropriate to say that he was "strange"; I myself might say
that he was "not normal." For example, a Zen master would normally
finish his training, have his own temple, and then teach his own
students. But when Bokuju finished his training, instead of entering
a temple, he decided to live in a barn.

Everyone knew that Bokuju was a fine priest, even though Bokuju
lived in a barn. Many monks in training came to Bokuju to engage
in Zen question and answer. Eventually Bokuju did have his own
temple. It was not unusual in those days for a famous Zen master
to have about five hundred students under him. There were roughly
three hundred students studying under Bokuju.

One day Zen Master Bokuju simply disappeared. This was
truly unusual, but it turned out that he wasn't up to anything too
strange. Bokuju had a very elderly mother and he wanted to be
with her. In China there is a strong moral principle that children

must take care of their parents and their siblings. So after studying for a long time as a Zen priest and trying hard to teach his own students as a Zen master, he found himself unable to leave his mother behind. Feeling he should be with her in her later years, he left the temple.

Bokuju made straw sandals out of hemp while living with his mother, and he sold them to support her. Bokuju's family name was "Chin." He was also called "straw sandals made out of hemp." Thus this rather unusual member of the Chin family made straw sandals to support his family. So while Bokuju was not quite normal, he was not exactly crazy. All things considered, we could say that he was simply eccentric.

Ummon learned about the famous Zen master Bokuju living in a barn and decided he would like to engage him with Zen question and answer. The fact that Bokuju kept the barn doors completely shut and they were extremely thick made this particularly challenging. Ummon declared that he wouldn't mind engaging in question and answer while the doors were shut; he would just call out what he wanted to ask. Bokuju would open the doors just a little bit and say, "Okay, spit it out." Most monks did not have the wherewithal to come up with an answer just like that, and would just stand and stare in utter shock. If a monk could not reply, Bokuju would open the door a little wider, grab the monk by his collar, shake him hard, push him down, and say, "This fellow had no purpose whatsoever." Then he would simply pop back into the barn, shut the door, and that was that.

Ummon decided to go to the barn and give it a try. The first time Ummon tried he didn't make it. He was blown away the second time as well. The third time the door opened up just a little bit. Seeing that if he couldn't get into the barn, he couldn't really engage in Zen question and answer, Ummon stuck his leg through the doorway just as Bokuju cracked it to say, "Okay, spit it out!" Since Ummon still didn't say anything, the door was slammed on his leg. That's how Ummon managed to have his leg broken. However, Ummon had his first satori enlightenment due to the extreme pain. Maybe you should try this yourself. You too might get satori!

Ummon later studied under Zen Master Seppo and became one of the great representatives of Southern Tang Zen. Ummon having his leg broken is one of the famous stories about him that my master told me when I was a novice in training. In my heart of hearts, I couldn't help thinking that Master Bokuju was a very bad teacher. I felt sympathy for Master Ummon. I thought it would have been better to just open the door and let Ummon in and engage in Zen question and answer. Then, if Bokuju simply taught Ummon well, he could lead him to enlightenment.

As a novice I thought Bokuju's teaching was wrong. But after studying Buddhism in college and studying Chinese Buddhism in graduate school, I finally engaged in real Zen training. I understood something for the first time when I entered the monastery to train: one trains very hard in the monastery. Friends in the monastery may not make the great effort needed to do zazen during the night sitting; they may just fall asleep. But I thought I should try to continue to sit as well as I could even during the night periods. That's when I reconsidered the story of Ummon's leg and realized that Master Bokuju was not really a bad master. I understood that just by sacrificing a leg, Bokuju was able to help Ummon gain his own satori enlightenment. I couldn't help but think that if that's what it takes to get satori enlightenment, then you should give up your legs, both legs, or both hands. I was able to continue night sitting with that kind of thinking.

As a novice I sympathized with Ummon. But when I actually began to train myself, I realized that Ummon did something brilliant. In sacrificing a leg, he gained satori enlightenment. Bokuju was a good Zen master, and Ummon was a very happy man after all. That is what I came to understand.

33

Fukei's Coffin, Ummon's Shit Stick, Tozan's Flax

A dirty thing is a dirty buddha. If you think Buddha is
only something pure and clean, you're mistaken.

THERE ARE MANY interesting stories about Zen Master Fukei.
When he thought he was about to die, the townspeople saw Fukei
carrying a coffin through town, calling out in a loud voice, "I think
I'll die at the east gate of town today." Wanting to see what would
happen, the townspeople gathered around the east gate. Once fifty
to a hundred people were following him, he said, "Well, maybe I'll
stop dying today." The next day he announced, "Today, I'm going to
die by the west gate." Once again many townspeople followed him.
But when he arrived at the west gate, he said, "I will not die today."
The third day he said he'd die by the south gate. The Chinese were
quite wonderful; again, on the third day, fifty to a hundred people
followed him, and when he arrived at the south gate, he announced
he would not die that day. Finally, on the fourth day, without saying
a word, he died at the north gate. A townsperson saw his coffin and
spread the news around town. The townspeople ran to the north gate
and opened the coffin, but there was no body inside. They wondered
where he went. They heard the sound of a small bell rolling along
somewhere. It rolled and rolled, and finally disappeared.

Whether or not this happened, I cannot really say. But there are many such stories about Zen Master Fukei. He was rather strange. I'd guess this story was invented after he lived.

Master Tozan was gathering kindling when a monk came to him and asked, "What is buddha nature?" Tozan answered, "Three pounds of flax." Tozan was expressing his own buddha nature in the same way that Master Joshu had done when he said, "An oak tree." A Japanese scholar set out to determine just how much three pounds of flax really was. In the China of Tozan's day, weights varied from time to time and place to place. It was a challenge for the scholar to determine exactly what three pounds of flax really amounted to during the Tang dynasty. In the end he did figure it out. But then he wondered why Tozan had said specifically three pounds. He could have said ten pounds of flax, a hundred pounds, or anything. Tozan's expression of three pounds of flax expressed his buddha nature, but it is also an excellent expression for another reason. If one has three pounds of flax, and works it into cloth, one can make robes for one human being. In other words, three pounds of flax means robes for one person; three pounds of flax is one person. Tozan ultimately means, "I am buddha nature"—a fine expression.

Zen Master Ummon was one of the great Zen masters living in southern China along the Yangtze River. He is famous for the phrase "Every day is a fine day." Once a monk asked Ummon, "What is buddha nature?" Ummon said, "A shit stick." Very dirty. Nowadays, when people think of Buddha, they envision a gold statue at the front of a temple, something pure and beautiful. This was also the case in the Tang dynasty. But given that we ourselves are buddha nature, there are all kinds of buddhas. Even Dirty Harry has buddha nature. It's good that there are many kinds of buddhas. Without understanding the true buddha nature within, we look for it outside. The monk who asked Ummon about buddha nature was attached to the image of a pure Buddha. Ummon used the image of something very dirty, a shit stick, to remove the monk's attachment. A dirty thing is a dirty buddha. If you think Buddha is only something pure and clean, you're mistaken.

While I was a novice in college, during vacations I'd return to my temple in the countryside to be with my master. He was very tall and I'm very short. He was quite proud of his height and was fond of saying that big is best. He'd say to me, "You're really short, aren't you?" I'd ask him why only tall things are good. He'd say, "Mount Fuji is big too." Because he was big, he liked big things. One day I was reading a book full of Zen sayings and found a phrase that said, "A tall person is a tall buddha, a small person is a small buddha." I thought, "Yeah! This is it!"

On my next vacation, I returned to my temple. I think my master was just waiting to tease me about being short. But the next time he said something, I replied, "Tall people are tall buddhas, small people are small buddhas." He never again told me I was short. Those who are tall are tall buddhas. If you're small you're just a small buddha. Men are men buddhas; women are women buddhas. There are American buddhas and Japanese buddhas. When you eat bread you're an eating buddha and when you drink coffee you're a drinking buddha. When I give a Dharma talk I'm a speaking buddha and everyone who listens is a listening buddha. This is how Zen represents the substantial form of buddha nature.

34

Kyogen's Tree

It's essential to have the first satori experience because it changes your world. But after you land, you must continue your journey to fully express satori with your whole life.

ZEN MASTER KYOGEN appears in Case 5 in the *Mumonkan*. Master Kyogen lived during the Tang dynasty. He was a man of excellent character and intelligence. Kyogen's master was Zen Master Isan. Kyogen trained hard under him, but he found it difficult to reach satori. Isan knew Kyogen was an excellent disciple, so he challenged him as follows: "Tell me what you have learned up to this point. Please do not answer using expressions from the sutras. Just give me one single, pure word of Zen from before you were born and before you knew anything about east and west." "Before you were born" means to transcend time, and "before you knew east from west" means to transcend space. Isan was asking Kyogen for a Zen expression that transcends time and space.

Kyogen was smart but Isan would accept none of his responses. So Kyogen asked Isan to please teach him. It is easy for someone with no deep Zen understanding to ask to be taught, but it takes real character for someone as far along as Kyogen to make such a request. If you think you already have great ability and knowledge, it's hard to ask someone else to teach you. Some people profess that they don't know anything, but they get upset if you agree with them. When the ego is involved, it's hard to ask someone to teach you. Kyogen's request to be taught showed the depth of his practice.

But Isan would not comply with Kyogen's request. "I could teach you," he said, "but if I did, it would be my mistake. It's up to you to say something in your own words." Facing this response, Kyogen gave up and left Isan. He set off on a journey. Along the way he visited the grave of one of his senior Dharma brothers, who was even older in the Dharma than Isan. The brother was Master Etsu, who is famous for having taught Zen to the Tang Emperor. At the grave, Kyogen made a decision that he couldn't reach satori and so would spend the rest of his life tending Etsu's grave. Kyogen's decision was not a trivial one. Every day he went to Etsu's gravesite to clean it. One day Kyogen was sweeping the dust from Etsu's grave, and there was a small pebble in with the dust. As Kyogen discarded the dust he'd gathered, the pebble fell, hit a piece of bamboo, and made a sound— *tock*! Kyogen reached satori when he heard the sound.

Kyogen and the sound of the pebble striking bamboo: there are many such cases. Mumon was enlightened at the sound of a drum. If you practice with deep concentration, you may one day suddenly attain satori like this. But it's not only sound that assists satori. Zen Master Reiun attained satori watching peach blossoms fall. Ummon attained satori when Master Bokuju slammed a heavy door on his leg. It was a vivid experience for Ummon, sacrificing a leg and reaching enlightenment. Master Gensha, who practiced with Ummon, attained satori when he hit his foot on a stone while walking in the mountains.

In terms of religious experience, when your state of mind grows very sharp, any circumstance can provoke enlightenment. Once Kyogen was enlightened by the sound of the pebble hitting bamboo, he was able to offer his own Zen words quite freely. He went back to

Isan's temple and, upon meeting Isan, made many deep bows and expressed how grateful he was that Isan had refused to tell him anything when he'd asked. Kyogen became a fine successor to Isan. He is known for the following story, which illustrates his strength as a teacher.

A person climbs a tree and is hanging by his teeth from a branch. His hands and legs are dangling and only his teeth gripping the branch holds him there. Someone approaches and asks, "What is Zen?" What would you do? Hanging in the tree and refusing to answer doesn't address the question to fulfill your spiritual responsibility, but saying even a single word will cause you to fall from the tree to the ground, perhaps even to your death.

Think about what you would do in such a situation. There are only two possibilities: you can keep hanging from the tree or you can open your mouth to answer and fall. What is Kyogen trying to teach about Zen with this story? Approaching the story intellectually, you see only two possibilities, but this is a limitation of the intellect. The real question is how you can give a Zen response. You either hang on to the branch with your teeth or open your mouth and fall. If you hang from the tree, you must become mushin hanging from the tree. You keep hanging, you must become mushin hanging. That's all. That's one possibility—hanging from the branch in mushin completely is one good Zen answer.

The second possibility is to open your mouth and fall out of the tree, which would be something like this: *Oouuuchiiii!* This is the experience of *ouch*! The concrete experience of hanging from the tree and the concrete experience of falling from the tree and feeling the pain is what Kyogen is teaching. Zen emphasizes raw experience. The samadhi of hanging on to the tree and the samadhi of pain falling from the tree are experiential facts. What Zen Master Kyogen was teaching is that if you realize you do not exist in these concrete experiences, that is satori. People often fall from trees or slip on the stairs, but such experiences don't normally include realization of no-self.

Hanging on to a tree isn't satori. Falling from a tree, feeling pain, and shouting "Ouch!" is also not satori. Satori isn't something strange. The question is whether or not you yourself realize the nature of no-self. This situation in Kyogen's story is imaginary, but it is a teaching filled with compassion. Zen emphasizes concrete down-to-earth experience: touch fire and it's hot; touch ice and it's cold. Zen teaches us to realize no-self in such concrete experience. This is always the theme of Zen: here, now, I myself.

Zen doesn't have to rely on invented cases like Kyogen's tree. When we sit, walk, eat, or read, no matter where we are or what we are doing, Zen is a matter of realizing no-self in such concrete experience. We must realize this no-self twenty-four hours a day, under all circumstances. When we discuss it like this, it sounds paradoxical. I tell you to concentrate on yourself, to be aware of yourself twenty-four hours a day. What happens to the self when you are aware of yourself? You realize no-self. You watch yourself, but the content of the watching is realizing that the self does not exist. It's complicated when we try to explain it with words, but as a concrete experience in one moment of time, it's not complicated. You watch this *self,* this *myself,* and in an instant you realize that you yourself do not exist. Experientially, you find the solution in an instant.

This is the first point of the satori experience in Zen. But this alone is not satori. It's only the foundation of satori, the fundamental satori. After such an experience, there's a great change. The world before satori and the world after satori are completely different. In 1969 a student in Claremont asked my master, Shibayama Roshi, "Is one satori experience enough?" My master said it is not. It's important to have one such experience, but that's not the end. Rather, it's the entrance to the world of satori after which you continue until you're dead. My master gave the following example. To get to Claremont, we would first fly to Los Angeles from Japan. Shibayama Roshi said that when the plane touched down on the runway in Los Angeles, this was like the first satori experience. After landing, some passengers would go east, some west. After landing, a great world unfolds. It's essential to have the first satori experience because it changes your world. But after you land, you must continue your journey to fully express satori with your whole life.

35

Tozan's Hot and Cold

"When you're cold, let the cold kill you. And when you're hot, kill yourself with heat." This is a very kind teaching, even though it doesn't sound that way.

ONE DAY a monk in training asked Tozan, the Tang dynasty Chinese Zen master, "When hot and cold arise, how do you escape them?" "Why don't you go to a world where there is no hot or cold?" Master Tozan answered.

Heat doesn't happen together with cold. It gets cold in the winter; it gets hot in the summer. I go to China almost every year. The Peking winter is very cold, but it's very hot in southern China at the same time. Tozan comes from China, so we can think of his reply as being based on the extremes of Chinese weather. The monk's question is, "When it gets cold in winter and hot in summer, how do you get beyond these extremes? How do you escape the physical suffering you feel in extreme heat or extreme cold?" So the monk is actually asking a question about duality. In reality we really do have hot and cold, don't we? So the question of how to get beyond hot and cold is really a question about how to transcend hot and cold while living with them.

Master Tozan's retort, "Why don't you go to a world where there is no hot or cold?" uses the expression "where there is no hot or cold." But in reality, no matter where we go, we are in a world of hot and cold. Even in the south, the winter gets cold in addition to being hot in the summer. This must even be true in the far north. It's not just cold there; it might get a little warm sometimes. By saying that you should go to a world where there's no hot or cold, Tozan actually meant that the monk needed to realize there really is no world without the feelings of hot and cold. Tozan is telling the monk he must transcend hot and cold.

This is Zen teaching. Because the monk's training was incomplete, he didn't understand. So he asked further, "Where is this world?" We can see just how undeveloped the monk's training really was based on his follow-up question. But Tozan offered another good teaching in response to it. So we're actually lucky that the monk asked it. Tozan said, "When you're cold, let the cold kill you. And when you're hot, kill yourself with heat." This is a very kind teaching, even though it doesn't sound that way.

What does it mean to kill ourselves with cold or heat? It means that when it's cold, we should become the cold. We should completely become the cold itself. And when it's hot, become the heat itself. It was a cold winter night outside last night, but I turned on the heat to warm it up inside. When I left and went outside, I could really feel the cold. When you feel the cold in such an instant, what is it? It's only, "Brrrr. It's cold!" Just like when you put your hand in the fire, there's nothing but the actual experience of heat.

Don't think that this means "I'm here in the hot room, then I go outside and it's I who feels the cold." Instead, when you open the door, go out, and feel the cold, "Brrrr, it's cold!" That's all there is! At that instant that's all there is—just the cold! The instant you become cold, there's nothing else. The instant you become the cold itself, there's no distinction between hot and cold, and it's the same when things are hot. Don't add all your thinking about yourself—"Oh, poor me!"—to the situation. Just meet it completely.

Why does Zen emphasize this point? It's because when you're able to use this kind of experience to realize no-self, that is satori enlightenment. It's not actually a case of realizing no-self. It's no-self that meets and realizes the cold. This is a concrete, actual experience. It's really the only experience there is, free from self-centered and extraneous thoughts. You may notice that it's no-self that feels the cold. In Zen we say it's no-self that becomes one with the cold in this moment. Someone who has had thorough Zen training will understand this.

Everything you feel, everything you see, everything you hear, everything you taste is real. A Zen priest focuses on what is real, what is concrete, what is actual. You should know hot and cold for yourself. No matter how much you may say about hot and cold, what you say is only an explanation. In Zen it is the experience of feeling the heat that is most important. Experience the cold that comes from touching ice. This is the way of the Zen priest in his everyday life, a way that emphasizes concrete experience. I have actually experienced minus-twenty-degree temperatures. It was the first time I experienced such cold. For a Zen master that was a very good experience.

Transcending dualities means becoming one with whatever you encounter. This transcendence is something you yourself practice and do. While living in a dualistic world, you transcend it, experience by experience. Wherever you go in the concrete world, everything is based on dualities. Let's live through the experience of becoming the duality we encounter and through the thought that it is possible to transcend duality by directly becoming it! Zen teaches this way of life.

Maybe the example of hot and cold isn't so good in this day and age. Hot and cold aren't so challenging anymore. We don't worry too much about hot and cold. Everyone has air conditioning. We could change the subject from hot and cold to life and death. If a monk asked Tozan, "When one encounters life and death, how do you escape this?" we realize he's not asking about a duality that can be removed from reality. All of us who are now living must eventually die. If we limit our thinking only to the question of hot or cold, we know that we can adjust the air conditioning to solve the problem. But there is no machine that eliminates death. Life and death is the great problem for us humans.

When we encounter life and death, how do we deal with it? If Tozan were here, he'd probably answer, "Why don't you go to a world where there is no life and death?" It's hard for us to understand the concept of no life and death, because there really are life and death in the real world. We must ask ourselves what it means to have a world where there is no life and death. Tozan would say, "When you're alive, let life kill you. When you die, kill yourself completely with death." I say "kill yourself completely" because in Zen "to kill" means to do something so thoroughly that self-consciousness is eliminated. Do things—do everything—that completely. While you're alive, be completely alive. And at the time of death, be completely dead. If you can understand this, it will be a very effective teaching for life. Let's live completely while we're alive! We should live completely in every moment.

What does it mean to live completely in every moment? Right now, as I'm composing this teaching, I should compose it as completely and fully as possible. You who are listening, listen completely. We should concentrate completely on what we're doing and experiencing in this moment. Realistically speaking, there are times when it's difficult to do that: when listening to the phone ring, when making tea, when looking after a child. There are times when we have to do many things all at once. What Zen teaches is that when we encounter such situations, we should always try, as a fundamental principle, to concentrate on one thing, but to include everything with complete presence.

Those who can live completely in this instant will be able to live completely for the whole day. Those who can live completely today will be able to do the same tomorrow. In this manner, day after day, they'll be able to live completely for a whole year. Year after year, they'll able to live a complete life. Having lived completely in this way, without being distracted from their lives, they will finally reach death. When it's time to die, they will just die completely. What other choice do we have?

Tozan's teaching of a world where there is no hot and cold directs us to live by transcending duality. By extension we can see that we need to concentrate completely on what we're doing, where we're doing it, and when we're doing it in the case of life and death. This is what Zen teaches about how to live, how to die, and how to resolve the duality of life and death.

Acknowledgments

WE WOULD LIKE TO THANK the many people who have helped to bring about this book. For their patient, skillful help with transcriptions of Fukushima Roshi's lectures we are grateful to Tom Hawkins, Sara Hunsaker, and Egyoku Nakao Roshi. Thanks also to John Merillat for his help with the transcripts and to Hide Yatabe for his translations of correspondence with friends and teachers in Japan.

We are also most grateful to our friends in Kyoto—to Zentaro Morioka and the Morioka family and to the Nishida family for their hospitality, to Professor K. Matsuura for his friendship and insight, to Jeff Shore for his hospitality and assistance, to the monks of Tofukuji monastery for their patience and kindness, to Professor Barbara Ruch for her dedication and generosity, and to Michikaku Mizutani of Sekisen Gallery for his assistance with Fukushima Roshi's calligraphy. And we especially wish to thank Harada Roshi, current abbot of Tofukuji, for his assistance.

Finally, our thanks to our kind and skillful editors at Wisdom, Andy Francis, Josh Bartok, and Brianna Quick.

Notes

1   Harris, Ishwar C., *The Laughing Buddha of Tofukuji: The Life of Zen Master Keido Fukushima* (Bloomington, IN: World Wisdom, 2004), 20.

2   Ongoing research, begun at Shasta Abbey, suggests that Hannyatara was a woman. Allegedly, Hannyatara and Bodhidharma met in Kerala, India's province of female gurus. Hannyatara's name in Sanskrit is feminine, and it is the only Indian Patriarch's name to reflect the feminine gender. Finally, teachers of Korean Zen have seen depictions of Hannyatara as a woman standing next to the Patriarch Bodhidharma depicted as a man. Further research is required to explore this interesting possibility. In the midst of Hannyatara being gifted with a beautiful jewel in this tale of meeting prince Bodhidharma, the possibility that Hannyatara may have been a woman could add context for the gift.

3   The usual translation of this phrase is "No, he does not ignore cause and effect." Shibayama offers the words *ignore, obscure,* and *evade* as potential translations of this phrase. Fukushima Roshi illustrates the transcendence of cause and effect through affirmation of relationship to cause and effect versus negation of the potential lack of applicability of the laws of cause and effect to an awakened being as the fox-monk had implied in his original answer.

About the Author

KEIDO FUKUSHIMA ROSHI trained under Zenkei Shibayama Roshi, one of the most famed Rinzai Zen masters of the twentieth century. Fluent in English, Fukushima Roshi had a special rapport with Western students, some of whom have become Zen teachers. He became head abbot of Tofukuji in Kyoto, making him the leader of one of the main Rinzai sects in Japan. He passed away in 2011.

About the Editors

MYOAN GRACE SCHIRESON is a Zen abbess and president of Shogaku Zen Institute (a Zen teachers' training seminary), and a clinical psychologist. She received Dharma transmission from Sojun Mel Weitsman Roshi of the Suzuki Roshi Zen lineage, and the late Fukushima Keido Roshi of Tofukuji monastery, Kyoto, asked her to teach the koan she studied with him during her practice there. She lives in California.

PETER SCHIRESON studied koans with Fukushima Roshi and is a Dharma heir in the Suzuki Roshi Soto Zen Lineage. He has had an active career in education and business and is a published poet. He lives in California.

What to Read Next
from Wisdom Publications

Zen Women
Beyond Tea Ladies, Iron Maidens, and Macho Masters
Grace Schireson
Foreword by Miriam Levering

"An exceptional and powerful classic with great depth, humor, and clarity."—Joan Halifax, abbess of Upaya Zen Center

Zen
The Authentic Gate
Koun Yamada
Foreword by David R. Loy

"Yamada's introduction to Zen is a welcome and dense primer that has much to offer novices as well as experienced practitioners."
—*Publishers Weekly*

The Zen Teaching of Homeless Kodo
Kosho Uchiyama and Shohaku Okumura
Edited by Molly Delight Whitehead

"Kodo Sawaki was straight-to-the-point, irreverent, and deeply insightful—and one of the most influential Zen teachers for us in the West. I'm very happy to see this book."—Brad Warner, author of *Hardcore Zen*

Novice to Master
An Ongoing Lesson in the Extent of My Own Stupidity
Soko Morinaga
Belenda Attaway Yamakawa

"This wise and warm book should be read by all."—Anthony Swofford, author of *Jarhead*

Moon by the Window
The Calligraphy and Zen Insights of Shodo Harada
Shodo Harada Roshi

"A gorgeous production. The calligraphy is some of the best I have ever seen and the remarks that go with each panel are deep and profound."—Mu Soeng, author of *The Heart of the Universe*

About Wisdom Publications

Wisdom Publications is the leading publisher of classic and contemporary Buddhist books and practical works on mindfulness. To learn more about us or to explore our other books, please visit our website at wisdompubs.org or contact us at the address below.

Wisdom Publications
199 Elm Street
Somerville, MA 02144 USA

We are a 501(c)(3) organization, and donations in support of our mission are tax deductible.

Wisdom Publications is affiliated with the Foundation for the Preservation of the Mahayana Tradition (FPMT).